# Video Kids

## Making Sense of Nintendo

Eugene F. Provenzo, Jr.

HARVARD UNIVERSITY PRESS
Cambridge, Massachusetts
London, England
1991

"Nintendo" is a registered trademark of Nintendo of America,
Incorporated, which has neither sponsored nor authorized
this book.

This book is printed on acid-free paper, and its binding
materials have been chosen for strength and durability.

Library of Congress Cataloging-in-Publication Data

Provenzo, Eugene F.
   Video kids : making sense of Nintendo / Eugene F. Provenzo,
Jr.
      p.    cm.
   Includes bibliographical references and index.
   ISBN 0-674-93708-2 (alk. paper).—
ISBN 0-674-93709-0 (pbk.)
   1. Video games—Social aspects.   2. Video games—Psycho-
logical aspects.   3. Nintendō Kabushiki Kaisha.
   4. Recreational surveys.
I. Title.
GV1469.3.P76   1991
794.8'1536–dc20         91-11697
                        CIP

*For David F. Baker*
in recognition of his significant contributions to the
development of the video game industry in America
and in appreciation of his insight and wisdom

## IMPORTANT
## NEW BOOKS

<u>DO NOT WRITE</u> IN THIS BOOK UNTIL YOU ARE CERTAIN YOU
<u>WILL NOT</u> HAVE TO RETURN IT. THE BOOK MUST BE IN
PERFECT CONDITION IN ORDER TO OBTAIN A REFUND. <u>NO</u>
REFUND AFTER 10TH CLASS DAY OF THE CURRENT COLLEGE
QUARTER REGARDLESS OF WHICH DAY YOUR CLASS FIRST
MEETS. <u>NO</u> REFUNDS WITHOUT A RECEIPT.

## USED BOOKS

> THERE IS NO GUARANTEE OF ANY RESALE
> VALUE OF THIS TEXTBOOK WHEN YOU ARE
> FINISHED USING IT.

USED BOOK BUYBACK IS CONDUCTED IN THE BOOKSTORE AT
THE <u>END</u> OF EACH QUARTER DURING FINALS. USED BOOKS
FROM PRIOR QUARTERS ARE <u>NOT</u> BOUGHT BACK BY THE
BOOKSTORE WHEN CLASSES RESUME.

THE AMOUNT PAID FOR USED BOOKS VARIES FOR THE
FOLLOWING REASON:

1. A NEW EDITION HAS BEEN PUBLISHED
   (MAKES PRIOR EDITIONS OBSOLETE USUALLY
   NO VALUE).

2. FACULTY ON THIS CAMPUS DID NOT REORDER
   TEXTBOOK FOR THE SUCCEEDING QUARTER.

3. THE BOOKSTORE HAS MORE COPIES OF THE
   TEXTBOOK THAN POTENTIAL CUSTOMERS.

IF THE BOOK HAS BEEN REORDERED FOR THE NEXT QUARTER,
THE AMOUNT PAID IS 50% OF THE NEW PRICE. REGARDLESS
OF WHETHER IT WAS NEW OR USED WHEN SOLD TO YOU.

IF THE BOOK <u>HAS NOT</u> BEEN REORDERED BY THE FACULTY
FOR THE NEXT QUARTER THE PRICE PAID IS A VALUE ESTAB-
LISHED BY USED BOOK DEALERS AND WILL ALWAYS BE LESS
THAN 50%.

BOOKS CAN STILL BE SOLD IF THEY ARE HIGHLIGHTED (NOT
TOO HEAVY), AND WORKBOOKS HAVE TO BE CLEAN. IT WILL
BE THE JUDGMENT OF THE BOOK BUYER AS TO THE RESALABLE
CONDITION OF THE TEXTBOOK.

# Contents

# Preface

Microcomputers have become an integral part of the world of childhood. Few elementary or secondary schools can be found that do not use microcomputers in their curriculum. Yet the presence of the computer in the classroom pales by comparison to the culture of computers and video games that has become so much a part of the day-to-day experience of many children. This book is an attempt to understand better the significance of video games as part of the culture and experience of childhood. It focuses on Nintendo—its world and the world of the children who play its games.

There are currently more than 19 million Nintendo game playing machines in the United States. The overwhelming majority of these game machines are owned by children. In addition to the games, there are Nintendo television programs, Nintendo books and magazines, Nintendo movies and video tapes, Nintendo lunch boxes, even Nintendo cereal, as well as social codes and traditions based on the Nintendo games and their characters.

Nintendo represents much more than just a video game system; it is also a profound cultural and media phenomenon. As Donald Katz observed in an article in *Esquire* ("The New Generation Gap," February 1990, p. 50): "Nintendo is like a '50s fantasy wedded with a '60s nightmare and '80s technology.

It's about actually getting inside the television and becoming one with it, being *of* it instead of outside looking in. Nintendo games call for good hand-eye coordination, and the capacity to handle myth, lore, a multitude of techniques, nuance, frustration, danger, betrayal, the fact that there's always somebody bigger and more powerful than you are, and the existential inevitability that—even if you kill the bad guys and save the girl—eventually you will die." Katz goes on to point out that Nintendo is wonderful from the point of view of children because it belongs to them. Nintendo is one of the great equalizers in the youth culture because it allows an eight-year-old to approach a fifteen-year-old and discuss something as peers. It is, according to Katz, "rock music and long hair and politics and even drugs back when they seemed okay."

In interviews with elementary school children that I conducted as part of the research for this book, the importance of Nintendo in the lives of many children was quite evident. A six-year-old kindergartner explained, for example, that she liked Nintendo "because it's fun! I don't like to play with my other toys that much, so I only play Nintendo. And I love the game too much, because I'm trying to get to another world where I have to come down with King Koppa, but he got me with spit and I ran out of time." There is an intensity in this little girl's description of her involvement in the microworld created while she plays Nintendo's *Super Mario Bros. 2* that that leads one to ask, why are children like her so passionate about video games?

In trying to answer this question, among others, I use an interdisciplinary approach in this book.

While it draws heavily on psychological literature, it is not a study in psychology. Instead, it represents a social and cultural analysis of the games and their meaning, with a largely qualitative approach. My hope is that the book will act as a catalyst for further discussion and research in the field. Many of the questions I touch on here, such as the long-term effect of video game playing on conceptions of self, whether video games encourage violence, and the effect of video games on gender relationships, go beyond the scope of this book and will require detailed longitudinal studies by psychologists. The question of the interaction between video games and other media such as television and film, though discussed in some detail in this work, also requires further exploration and analysis. My intention is to alert researchers, as well as parents, teachers, and the public in general, to the power of Nintendo as a social, cultural, and educational phenomenon, and to gain a better understanding of what the "world of Nintendo" is actually about.

Many people have contributed to the writing of this book. Special thanks go to Carmen Fajardo for leading me to think about some of the issues raised here. The administrators, teachers, parents, and students of the West Laboratory School were particularly generous in allowing me to explore the world of Nintendo with them. A number of my colleagues at the University of Miami, including Brookes Applegate, Arlene Brett, Jack Coffland, Maria Llabre, Marjorie Montague, and Liz-Christman Rothlein, contributed insights about computers. I also had helpful discussions with Lauren Hughes, Don Meagher, and

Brainard Hines. A sabbatical from the School of Education, University of Miami, during the spring of 1990 allowed me the time to complete a first draft of this book.

Cheryl Mell, Julie de Castro, and Mike Hurley are to be thanked for gathering research materials for the project. Dorothy Rosenthal and her staff in the Interlibrary Loan Department, Otto G. Richter Library, University of Miami, were especially helpful in tracking down sources. Sylvia and David Romero and Teresa Pacin lent me equipment and games and shared their insights into the world of Nintendo. Thanks also go to the manager and staff at Spec's Music and Video in Coral Gables, Florida.

I would especially like to thank Victor Dover of Image Network, Inc., Coral Gables, Florida, and John T. Reagan, Dean of the School of Design at North Carolina State University, as well as Michael Greenberg, David F. Baker, and Asterie Baker Provenzo, who are always eager to discuss the excitement of computers and video games and their impact on our lives.

Finally, I want to thank some children of friends and neighbors who let me become part of their world and the world of Nintendo: Michael and Gabriel Hines; Lolly, Henry, and Rama Hughes; and, of course, the kids down the street—Christina and Paul Fajardo.

# Video Kids

# Introduction

It is early Saturday afternoon in a multi-screen theater at the Miracle Center on Coral Way in Miami—just a week before Christmas. School let out yesterday for the holidays. The theater is full of children and their parents.

Opposite the candy counters are rows of video arcade games. Most of the games are based on recent movies: *Willow, RoboCop,* and *Back to the Future.* The machines are surrounded by groups of young boys between the ages of eight and twelve. They stand in quiet concentration, watching whoever is "on the machine."

There is no roughhousing or joking around while they play the games. One can sense the intensity of the children playing and of those in the group watching, as joysticks are pushed and pulled and buttons pressed and slammed. The games, with their simulated combat, martial-arts motifs, and themes focusing on quests and adventures, are taken very seriously.

In the background—distanced from the video games—are several mothers. They wait patiently, if hesitantly, as their sons take their turns at the machines. It is only the announcement that the movie is about to begin that finally allows them to pull their children away from the games and go into the theater.

The movie that is being shown is *The Wizard*, starring Fred Savage, Jenny Lewis, Christian Slater, and Luke Edwards. It is the story of a six- or seven-year-old boy named Jimmy Woods who has been traumatized by the accidental death of his twin sister. Barely speaking and psychologically isolated, he resists the efforts of his parents to reach out to him and does not respond to the treatment of psychologists. Finally he is institutionalized by his mother and stepfather, with whom he lives. Having experienced a major tragedy, separated from his biological father and brothers, Jimmy is an isolate, suffering deeply from the misfortunes imposed on him by life. He is also a child who is searching for a meaning to his life.

This quest for meaning is expressed by Jimmy in a number of ways. Early in the film, after having run away and been returned by the police to his mother and stepfather, he is left to play in a psychologist's office. While being observed through one-way mirrors by the psychologist and his mother and stepfather, he constructs towers and buildings that are highly repetitive in their shape. The psychologist explains Jimmy's behavior by saying that "he is searching for a way to express himself." As the film unfolds, it is not building with blocks but the world of video games—specifically the symbolic culture of Nintendo—that ultimately provides Jimmy the means by which to express and to "discover himself."

Jimmy's eleven- or twelve-year-old brother Corey, who lives alone with their biological father, finds out that Jimmy has been institutionalized in a special school and decides to rescue him. In the process of escaping from the school, Jimmy and Corey meet up with a street-smart little girl about Corey's age named Haley. By this point in the movie, Corey has discovered that Jimmy has a phenomenal ability to play video games. He and Haley hatch up a plan to take Jimmy to Los Angeles to compete in a video game competition—"Video Armageddon."

The main part of the movie focuses on the children's adventures as they try to reach Los Angeles for the video game competition. They are pursued by Jimmy's father and brother, and by a sleazy private detective hired by Jimmy's mother and stepfather, whose specialty is tracking down runaway children. Corey and Haley finance the trip by hustling unsuspecting marks to play video games against Jimmy.

The most formidable opponent they meet on their trip is Lucas, a handsome, super-cool twelve- or thirteen-year-old, whose video game ability is described by the kids in the isolated desert town where he lives as being "awesome." The owner of ninety-seven video games, Lucas clearly has vast knowledge of the games and of their tricks and intricacies.

As Lucas prepares to take his turn at a road racing game in a video game showdown with Jimmy, a series of complex auditory and visual images and associations appear on the movie screen. Lucas, for example, slowly pulls out a secret weapon—a Nintendo Entertainment System "Power Glove." The Power Glove is a new type of joystick or computer controller based on the principles of "virtual reality,"[1] where the player can control the action on the screen by moving his hand in the glove. As Lucas dons the glove, the film's soundtrack plays a subtle chord of Western gunslinger music. As he punches up the control panel on his glove, the computerized theme from the science fiction movie *Close Encounters of the Third Kind* is heard.

Lucas is a Samurai warrior, the Ninja martial arts expert, the gunslinger with his six-shooter. Style is a critical part of his success, as he artfully makes his moves through the computer race game. On completing the game with what is clearly an extremely high score, he looks at Corey and says: "I love the Power Glove. It's so bad." Jimmy is completely overwhelmed by Lucas, his skill and his expert knowledge. He knows nothing about the new technology of the Power Glove and refuses to play Lucas. The film's dramatic tension increases when the kids discover that Lucas is also on his way to compete at the video game competition in Los Angeles.

Despite his failure to meet Lucas's challenge, Jimmy goes on to Los Angeles with Corey and Haley. Along the way they stop in Reno, where they raise more money for their trip by convincing an older friend to successfully shoot craps for them—the older friend taking cues from Haley. Meanwhile, Jimmy carefully practices video games at a local arcade. Haley takes on the role of researcher and coach, calling up the Nintendo Hot Line in order to provide Jimmy with inside information on how to play the games—evidently receiving secret and specialized information that is critical if they are to defeat Lucas.

Finally arriving in Los Angeles, they go to Universal Studios where, after a series of adventures and narrow escapes, Jimmy competes in the contest. In the finals, which of course include Lucas and Jimmy as opponents, the boys are presented with a totally new game to play, Nintendo's *Super Mario Bros. 3*. Faltering during the early part of the game, Jimmy takes advantage of a "Magic Star" at a crucial moment in the game in order to move to a higher level. In the end, he is victorious both in the game and in overcoming his withdrawal from the world. Nintendo has been the instrument of his salvation.

As people leave the theater after the movie, the ushers hand them a copy of a magazine entitled *Pocket Power*. Jimmy is pictured on the front of the magazine standing in front of the computer controls for the Video Armageddon competition. He is looking at the words "The Wizard," which are presented in a highly stylized format. Underneath them is a video screen on which he is outlined in phosphorescent green.

Jimmy's computer image on the video screen is extremely revealing. With his arms and legs outstretched, he is surrounded by a circle and square. Obviously the image is based on Leonardo Da Vinci's anatomical drawing of a man—perhaps the quintessential image in many people's minds of the "Renaissance man." Through his mastery of the Nintendo games, Jimmy has become a *cognoscente* or master—a fully realized intellect and human being in the Renaissance tradition.

Included in the magazine is a short article on *The Wizard* and its star, Fred Savage. Advertisements for *Wizard* T-shirts, posters, and lunch boxes are included, as well as advertisements for various Nintendo games such as *Duck Tales, RoboCop, Dragon Warrior, Double Dragon, The Chessmaster, Stealth, Fester's Quest, Marble Madness, Snake's Revenge, Double Dragon II,* and *Super Mario Bros. 3.* Advertisements for subscriptions to the magazine *Nintendo Power* explain to the reader: "If you don't get Nintendo Power magazine, then you just can't win. Nintendo Power is the *official* source for your Nintendo Entertainment System (NES) and Game Boy. It's direct from the pros at Nintendo. Only *they* know all the inside secrets."[2] Announcements are included for the 1990 Nintendo World Championships. A double-page advertisement at the conclusion of the magazine introduces the Power Glove, declaring that "Everything Else Is Child's Play."[3] It explains that with the glove: "You actually knock out Mike Tyson. Grab the steering wheel of Rad Racer . . . Twist your wrist for an immediate head butt in Double Dragon. Bend a finger for "Thrash Mode"—your character turns and shoots in all possible directions."[4] The advertisement concludes: "It's the future of video games. Years ahead of schedule. So put on the Power Glove and put on the power of the future. And feeling everything else become child's play."[5]

Many elements of *The Wizard*—its blatant commercialism, violent games, tricks, secrets, and codes; its elaborate video game equipment and symbolism; the young people seeking fulfillment and self-knowledge through simulated and real adventures—are part of the world of Nintendo. This book is a detailed examination of this world, in which I attempt to understand the meaning of Nintendo and its importance in the lives of children. Although other video game systems such as Sega or Activision could have provided the focus for this study, I have chosen Nintendo as the main subject of this book because of its overwhelming domination of the video game field and because of what I have come to believe is its power as a social, cultural, and educational phenomenon.

# 1

## The Video Game Market

The major force in the current video game market is the Japanese company Nintendo. Nintendo first introduced its hardware system in 1986.[1] By June of 1988 it had sold 11 million units. In 1990 there were 7.2 million Nintendo entertainment systems sold, and total sales for the Nintendo Corporation amounted to $3.4 billion. Total sales for the video game industry as a whole in 1990 were $4 billion.[2] Undoubtedly encouraged by Nintendo's success, seven other companies were marketing major game systems by 1988.[3]

Although Nintendo is overwhelmingly the single most popular video game system introduced in America in recent years, video games are by no means a new phenomenon but date back nearly two decades. The current wave of interest in video games can be traced back to the early 1970s. In 1972 Atari introduced *Pong,* an electronic table-tennis game. Within a year, over 6,000 of the games were sold nationwide at a cost of more than $1,000 each. An additional

9,000 games were manufactured under license by Midway Manufacturing Company. In the same year Magnavox introduced a video game system, Activision, that could be played on home television sets. By the end of 1976 over twenty different companies were producing video games for home use.[4]

In 1976 Fairchild Camera and Instrument entered the video game field with the first programmable video game system. This system used an electronic cartridge that was plugged into a game console, thus making it possible to play as many different games as there were game cartridges. By 1978, Americans were spending more than $200 million per year on programmable home video games. By 1981 this figure had grown to $1 billion per year.[5]

The development of the home video game market took place simultaneously with a series of developments in other computer-related fields. In 1977 the Apple II computer was introduced commercially, setting in motion a revolution in personal or home computing. Video arcade games swept the nation a short time later, offering innovative game scenarios and much higher quality graphics and action than had been available on the earlier home video game systems. By 1982, a total of $8 billion was being spent per year on video arcade games in the United States.[6] Home video games represented a $3 billion market.[7]

By the mid-1980s, it appeared that the home video game market had, as one analyst put it, "crashed and burned."[8] Sales reached a low of $100 million in 1985. The introduction of new systems such as Nintendo, however, brought sales up to $430 million in

*Table 1.1*  Annual sales figures for the video game industry

| Year | Annual sales |
| --- | --- |
| 1979 | $330 million |
| 1980 | $446 million |
| 1981 | $1 billion |
| 1982 | $3 billion |
| 1983 | $2 billion |
| 1984 | $800 million |
| 1985 | $100 million |
| 1986 | $430 million |
| 1987 | $1.1 billion |
| 1988 | $2.3 billion |
| 1989 | $3.4 billion |
| 1990 | $4 billion |

*Sources:* Donna Leccese, "Video Games Go Back to the Future," *Playthings,* June 1988, p. 33; Teresa Salas, "Video Game Market Continues to Shine," *Playthings,* January 1990, p. 39; "Nintendo Scored Record Sales in 1990," *The Miami Herald,* January 11, 1991.

1986, $1.1 billion in 1987, $2.3 billion in 1988, $3.4 billion in 1989, and $4 billion in 1990 (Table 1.1).[9]

## Home Video Games in the Late 1980s

The home video game systems recently introduced by companies such as Nintendo, Activision, and Sega are different from their predecessors. These systems plug into a television and include hand controllers that are used to manipulate the action on the screen. The games are included on removable cartridges. These new systems offer faster character movement, more realistic sound effects, and a host of add-on accessories all aimed at keeping up with the tastes of the primary target audience—boys, ages eight to eighteen.[10]

Chris Garske, general manager for video games at Activision, breaks down their software into four categories: (1) action/adventure, (2) action/arcade, (3) simulation, and (4) sports. A fifth area that is emerging is strategy, which is focused more on the potential adult market.[11]

Market analysts account for the resurgence of the video game industry as being the result of a new generation of children reaching game-playing age. According to Michael Katz, video games reached a saturation point in 1982 when more than 30 million game systems had been sold. Since there were 35 million households with children of ages six to sixteen, "the market had no place to go. Now, however, there is a new generation of 154 million households with children that have never had video."[12] Other reasons for the resurgence in the industry have to do with improvements in hardware and software, including lower prices for more sophisticated equipment.

The importance of Nintendo for the toy industry and of the revival of the video game market in the late 1980s cannot be overemphasized. Describing the sales conditions for the toy industry in 1987, Michael Katz, president of Atari's electronic division, explained that "without video games last year, most of the toy retailers would have broken even, or taken a slight loss." According to Katz, "in some cases, video hardware and software accounted for as much as 25 to 30 percent of a toy chain's total first quarter volume. The importance of the category to key retailers is tremendous."[13]

In order to understand the extent to which video games have come to dominate the toy industry in recent years, one need only look at the retail sales figures for toys in the United States. For February 1989, 16 of the 20 top selling toys in the country were video games or video game–related. These included:

1. *Action Set* (Nintendo of America)
2. *Power Set* (Nintendo of America)
3. *Nintendo Paper Boy* (Mindscape)
4. *Nintendo Simon's Quest* (Konami)
5. *Nintendo Skate or Die* (Ultra Software)
6. *Nintendo Pac Man* (Tengen Inc.)
7. *Advantage Joystick* (Nintendo of America)
8. *Super Mario Bros. 2* (Nintendo of America)
9. *Nintendo Town & Country Surf* (LJN)
10. *Nintendo WWF Wrestling* (Acclaim Entertainment)
14. *ProAm Racing* (Nintendo of America)
15. *Legend of Zelda* (Nintendo of America)
16. *Anticipation* (Nintendo of America)
17. *Nintendo Xenophobe* (Sun Corp. of America)
18. *Nintendo Mickey Mouse* (Nintendo of America)
20. *Nintendo Metal Gear* (Ultra Software Corp.)[14]

Video games and equipment also dominated sales figures for the toys listed as the best-selling items for retailers in the 21st to 30th positions. Video-related toys included:

21. *Nintendo Double Dribble* (Konami)
22. *Nintendo Rampage* (Data East)

23. *Nintendo Top Gun* (Konami)
24. *Ice Hockey* (Nintendo of America)
25. *Super Mario Bros.* (Nintendo)
26. *Sega Master System* (Sega)
27. *7800 game system* (Atari)
28. *Nintendo Contra* (Konami)
30. *Bubble Bobble* (Taito America)[15]

Thus, of the 30 best selling toys in America, 25 were either video games or video game equipment.

For the Nintendo Entertainment System, the average price of each game is about $40. They are rarely discounted. In 1988, total sales for Nintendo systems and related licensed merchandise (clothing, board games, dolls, and so forth) reached $1.7 billion. According to Nintendo spokespersons, 12 percent of all American homes owned Nintendo systems.[16] By the middle of 1989, Nintendo commanded approximately 80 percent of the video game market.[17] As one market analyst has explained: "Some call it a retailer's dream: a heavily pre-sold product that promotes itself, uses no advertising dollars, and is presently riding the wave of intense popularity."[18] Nintendo and its competitors are clearly a force to be reckoned with in the toy industry. During the 1987, 1988, and 1989 Christmas seasons, Nintendo was the single largest selling toy. Of the estimated $11.4 billion spent on toys in 1989, 23 percent of the total was for Nintendo products.[19]

## Adolescents and the Video Game Market

Nintendo, like other video hardware and game manufacturers, is particularly sensitive to the youth and adolescent consumer market. While interested in expanding its markets into a larger demographic sector, the company is profoundly aware that its main audience is the youth market. According to Peter Main of Nintendo of America: "The positioning of our company has been one of total family entertainment, that we initially got to by going after boys 8 to 15, the traditional heavy users of home video. But two years later, as we examined demographics of the primary users, the biggest group of primary users continues to be boys in that 8 to 11 group, accounting for about 36 percent of our total users, and the second biggest group, just a point and a half behind that, are adults 18 plus."[20] Children under six years of age account for fewer than 2 percent of Nintendo's primary users.[21]

According to Tom Panelas, a communication and media researcher interested in video games, this eight- to fifteen-year-old age group reflects "the existing symbiosis between the social life of teenage peer groups and the marketing practices of popular culture and leisure industry. From the industry's point of view, the essential ingredient of this relationship is the linkage of cultural products with a population subgroup whose general tastes are known, relatively homogeneous, but highly changeable."[22] Products such as video games are culturally and socially appropriated, according to Panelas, taking on symbolic value among their users.[23] It is not surprising, therefore, that product markets expand beyond the video games themselves into a whole range of media and consumer products associated with games.

The extent to which Nintendo's product market has been expanded can be seen in the wide range of secondary products that have been licensed by the company. General Foods, the manufacturer of Jell-O

Frozen Snacks, is a co-sponsor of the 1990 Nintendo World Championships. Oreo Cookies include Nintendo stickers and contests with their product, and the Ralston Purina Company actually markets a "Nintendo Cereal System." Two bags of cereal are included in each "System" box: one contains green and yellow pieces of cereal that represent figures from the *Zelda* Adventure Series, and the other, yellow, red, and blue pieces of cereal that represent characters from the *Super Mario Bros.* Action Series.

Illustrations from game screens are included on the side of the Nintendo cereal box, as well as "game tips" for playing both *Super Mario Bros. 2* and *Zelda II (Link)*. Inside the cereal box are free Nintendo stickers and an opportunity to win a Nintendo Power Glove "instantly." "Top Secret Tips" are found inside the cereal box as well. For the game *Super Mario Bros. 2*, a printed card explains: "There is a good deal of quicksand in World Two (notice that the grains move in a wave motion). Keep jumping and you won't get sucked under!"[24] As mentioned earlier, Nintendo lunch boxes, sweat shirts and T-shirts, watches, movies, posters, sleeping bags, dolls, wallpaper, trophies, and magazines are just a few examples of the products created by the company—products that have symbolic importance extending significantly beyond their utilitarian function for the cultural subgroup that buys them.

The distribution of commercial products related to video games provides an important case study of the relationship between cultural groups and leisure products. Questions arise as to how a product such as Nintendo creates an identifiable cultural subgroup within our society—one held together through game playing, common cultural figures (Mario, Teenage Mutant Ninja Turtles, Zelda, Bionic Man, Mega Man, and so on), and shared consumption. Referring back to the work of Daniel Boorstin, Panelas argues that video games represent an important type of socially coded goods around which cultural allegiances can be developed.[25] According to Panelas, "Much of what passes as symbolic communality among large and geographically dispersed subcultures is based primarily on consumption patterns."[26]

Related to the creation of consumer markets focused around socially coded goods is the creation of expert knowledge about these products. In the case of Nintendo, an entire subfield within the computer video game industry involving the distribution of this expert knowledge has developed. Books such as *How to Win at Nintendo Games #2* provide the reader with "secret codes," "training tips," and "expert tactics" for games such as *Adventure Island, Bionic Commando, Blaster Master, Double Dragon, Section Z, Teenage Mutant Ninja Turtles, Seicross, Superman,* and *ZANAC,* to name just a few.[27] As the advertisement on the back of the book asks:

> Is vidscreen victory eluding you? Be vanquished no more! Jeff Rovin—the vidgame expert who brought you the first-ever survival guide to Nintendo—now shows you more tactics, techniques and specs of 30 of the most popular video games not covered in his first book . . . this-easy-to-use guide breaks each game into twenty sections with such information as:
> - Layout of each game
> - Patterns of scenery, obstacles
> - What you must decimate, defeat, or discover to score
> - Ratings of difficulty, graphics, sound effects
> - And much more[28]

Magazines such as *Game Player's* feature "games thoroughly examined with page after page of full-color maps, strategy hints and tips, and screen shots."[29] Nintendo Corporation of America publishes its own bimonthly magazine, *Nintendo Power,* which offers hot tips, game reviews and previews, expert tricks, and secret clues.[30] Telephone 1-900-hotlines provide expert advice on playing the games at $1.25 for the first question and $.75 for each subsequent question, while the *Official Game Player's Gametapes* "provide valuable hints and tips for four or more games." These tapes include "easy-to-follow, step-by-step instructions from our expert game players. Actual game footage shows you how to get through difficult spots, and provides tips on how and where to find hidden power-ups, treasures, weapons and other important items."[31]

## Linking of Games to the Larger Media

Nintendo has been remarkably successful at linking its video games not only to current mass media themes, but also to historically powerful themes as well. Among the more popular videotape cartoons rented by children in the last few years have been the Disney *Duck Tales*. The *Duck Tales* are based on the adventures of Uncle Scrooge and his nephews, Huey, Dewey, and Louie, a highly popular comic book series since the 1950s. By developing an adventure game around the Uncle Scrooge figure, Nintendo is able immediately to tap into an enormously popular cultural and symbolic tradition—thus making its own product all the more commercially viable.

Similar approaches have been taken with the

World Wrestling Federation's champion Hulk Hogan. Hogan, who has become a widely recognized popular culture figure in recent years, is regularly seen on television, endorses a wide range of products, and has a considerable following among both children and adults. In an advertisement included in the June/July 1989 issue of *Game Player's* for the game *Wrestlemania,* the reader is told: "You've always dreamed of being Hulk Hogan. Or one of the other WWF Superstars. And now here's your chance. Challenge your opponent to a wild match of dropkicks, headlocks, bodyslams and more! Or create your own tournament and compete against your friends or the computer. Up to six can play. So step into the ring and experience WWF Wrestlemania . . . from the inside!"[32] Other Nintendo games are based on widely popular sports figures, including *Jordan vs. Bird: One on One, Magic Johnson's Fast Break,* and *Mike Tyson's Punch-Out!!*

Recently, television programming based on Nintendo game characters has become popular. The *Super Mario Brothers Show,* for example, is a half-hour adventure/cartoon show in which live actors playing the roles of Mario and his brother Luigi act out various skits and introduce a daily cartoon based on the Mario Brothers characters or the characters found in the video game *The Adventure of Zelda.* Children's products including cereal, snacks, and video games are advertised during the program.

Movies popular with the youth market are rapidly adapted as video games. *RoboCop,* a highly popular science fiction movie about a half-human and half-robot police officer in Detroit, has recently been released as a video game. In an advertisement for the game included on the back cover of *Game Player's* magazine, we learn that

THE FUTURE OF LAW ENFORCEMENT HAS ARRIVED. Detroit has seen better days. A gang of ruthless hoods has overrun the city, and crime is out of control. Attacks on the street. Drug trafficking. Corruption and cop killing. It is so bad a private firm, O.C.P., now runs the police department. As RoboCop, your job is simple—clean up the city. Armed with a heavy-duty arsenal of weapons, including RoboCop's Special Issue Auto-9, make your way past street thugs, the notorious Clarence Boddicker and the powerful ED-209 to your final battle with Dick Jones.[33]

Other films on which Nintendo games have been based include *Willow, Who Framed Roger Rabbit, Predator, Platoon, Friday the 13th, Back to the Future, Indiana Jones and the Temple of Doom,* and *Ghostbusters.* Television programs are also represented in video games, such as *Sesame Street ABC, Sesame Street 1, 2, 3, The Three Stooges, Airwolf,* and *Fester's Quest,* which is based on the character Uncle Fester from the program *The Addams Family.* Cartoon figures also appear, such as Charles Schultz's Snoopy in *Snoopy's Silly Sports Spectacular* and Bugs Bunny in *Bugs Bunny's Crazy Castle.*

In the interviews and surveys conducted with children at the West Laboratory School for this book (see Appendix A), there is overwhelming evidence to indicate that video games, television, and motion pictures are increasingly linked with one another. Four of the ten most popular television programs listed by children in grades 1 through 6 at the school were based on video games; these included *Teenage*

*Mutant Ninja Turtles, Chip and Dale Rescue Rangers,* the *Mario Brothers Super Show,* and *Duck Tales* (Table 1.2). Although these figures are limited to a single school, it is probably reasonable to assume that they are typical for other parts of the country.

Even media that do not have an immediate connection with video games are used to promote them. Popular youth and adolescent television figures are

*Table 1.2*  Tabulations of students' three favorite television programs, grades 1–6, West Laboratory School

| Programs | Grades | | | | | | Totals |
|---|---|---|---|---|---|---|---|
| | 1 | 2 | 3 | 4 | 5 | 6 | |
| *The Simpsons* | — | 1 | 1 | 6 | 14 | 25 | 47 |
| *Teenage Mutant Ninja Turtles** | 11 | 13 | 12 | 5 | 2 | — | 43 |
| *Full House* | 6 | 10 | 4 | 1 | 9 | 2 | 32 |
| *Cosby Show* | — | 4 | 5 | 5 | 13 | 3 | 30 |
| *America's Funniest Home Videos* | 1 | 3 | 3 | — | 2 | 12 | 21 |
| *In Living Color* | — | — | — | 1 | 6 | 12 | 19 |
| *Chip and Dale Rescue Rangers** | 7 | 4 | 4 | 3 | — | — | 18 |
| *Mario Brothers Super Show** | 3 | 5 | 6 | 3 | — | — | 17 |
| *Family Matters* | 3 | 6 | — | — | 3 | — | 12 |
| *Duck Tales** | 2 | 4 | 3 | 2 | — | — | 11 |

*Note:* The sample was a 50% random sample for grades 1–5, total population for grade 6.

*Television program that has either a video game theme or a video game based on the program.

frequently found promoting the games in articles included in various magazines. It is probably no accident that Fred Savage, the popular star of the television program *The Wonder Years,* was chosen as the main character for the movie *The Wizard.*

A specific example of how television stars are promoted as video game players in game magazines can be seen in the case of Danny Pintauro. Pintauro, who played the role of Jonathan Bower in the ABC television series *Who's the Boss,* is quoted at length in the magazine *Game Player's* about his favorite games: "*Rampage* is my all-time favorite game because it is challenging. I have destroyed the U.S.A. on *Rampage,* so I guess that I had a pretty high score. I would like to see a new version of *Rampage* developed, where the player has to destroy the whole world, not just the United States."[34] Various aspects of Pintauro's career, a discussion of his favorite game controller, and his summertime activities fill out the article.

Another example of celebrity promotion can be found in an article in the January/February 1989 issue of *Nintendo Power* that gives a profile of the captain of the 1984 and 1988 U.S. Olympic volleyball teams, Karch Kiraly; there is also a description of how members of the American Olympic volleyball team took a Nintendo system to an international meet in the Soviet Union, as well as to the Olympic Games in Seoul, South Korea. Nintendo games owned by Kiraly and his wife are listed in the article.[35]

By connecting media information and cultural figures to video games—particularly popular actors or sports figures—the user is able to associate the game and himself with an alter ego: Karch Kiraly,

Danny Pintauro, Fred Savage, and so on. In the case of the movie *Predator,* for example, the player is able to hunt the alien just as the Arnold Schwarzenegger character did. Sherry Turkle in her book *The Second Self* argues in the context of video arcade games that such an approach "is custom made for the computer generation: you identify with an alter ego as you play your role in the dungeon, but the process of play is mathematical and procedural. Beyond the fantasy, there are always the rules."[36] Additional questions are raised by Turkle concerning what happens to the individual as he enters into the simulation and assumes the role of the movie character or sports figure. In this process, there is more than simply an identification with the character on the screen. As she explains:

> When you play a video game you enter into the world of the programmers who made it. You have to do more than identify with a character on the screen. You must act for it. Identification through action has a special kind of hold. Like playing a sport, it puts people into a highly focused, and highly charged state of mind. For many people, what is being pursued in the video game is not just a score, but an altered state.[37]

Turkle describes this altered state as literally being a "second self." This idea of a second self is an extremely important point. Video games, as I will attempt to demonstrate, are not neutral but value-laden. The commercial promotion of these games creates a situation in which there is not only a "contact between the physical child and the physical machine," but "between the child's culture and a culture of simulation."[38] Significantly, as Turkle points out, in contrast to the world of sports or literature, or even pinball, the computers upon which the video games are based ultimately make them "rule-driven"—that is, they incorporate the rules by which they are programmed.[39]

In the end, the content of video games such as those included as part of the Nintendo system and their connection to media sources can provide us with important insight into the values and beliefs that permeate American culture and society. As Terri Toles explains in his article "Video Games and American Military Ideology":

> It is easy enough to dismiss the video game subculture as simply an element of popular culture that has little real meaning in a complex society. Yet, the games provide important clues to the values and beliefs central to our culture. The world created by play and games allows for a subtle expression of the ways of perceiving consensual reality held by a culture. Games serve as extensions of social man, giving new meaning to social structures that have become so familiar that their meaning is forgotten or obscured as we conduct the routine activities of everyday life.[40]

Arguments such as these assume that video games are important social and cultural statements. In the following section I analyze Nintendo's importance as a financial force within the video game industry, and, by implication, the significance of video games as a cultural and social force.

## Nintendo's Monopoly of the Video Game Market

The Nintendo Corporation overwhelmingly dominates the contemporary video game market in America. It has been accused by numerous sources of systematically cornering this market. Early in December of 1989, for example, Representative Dennis Eckhart, a Democrat from Ohio and chairman of the House Small Business Subcommittee on Antitrust, requested that the Justice Department's antitrust division investigate Nintendo's American subsidiary, Nintendo Incorporated of America. According to Eckhart, Nintendo has intimidated retailers to keep competitors' games off toy store shelves, has used exclusive software arrangements and physical computer chip barriers to control the video game market, and has created artificial shortages of some games sold by licensed software producers in order to ensure continued demand.[41] According to Eckhart: "They have done a brilliant job in marketing their product, but the simple fact remains that our subcommittee investigation has revealed there is no competition among competitors . . . Nintendo right now is saying you can buy our machines but you can play only our games."[42]

Although Nintendo officials angrily denied Eckhart's charges, there is considerable evidence to support the claims of his subcommittee. Nintendo, for example, has established guidelines for games used on its hardware that require all software developed by third-party software designers to be exclusive to the Nintendo system. In addition, all software must be approved by the company before it can be released and must be manufactured by Nintendo.[43] Ostensibly, Nintendo has taken control in an attempt to avoid the flooding of the game cartridge market that led to the collapse of video game sales in 1983. Its actions have also had the effect of monopolizing the content and type of games made available to the market.

Nintendo has been involved in numerous lawsuits as part of an attempt to maintain its dominance in the video game market. In August of 1989, for example, Nintendo succeeded in obtaining an injunction against the Blockbuster Entertainment chain of video rental stores to stop them from copying and distributing Nintendo instruction manuals. While claiming copyright infringement, Nintendo was in fact attempting to prevent the rental of its video games, which by itself is not illegal. Nintendo has unsuccessfully lobbied Congress to pass legislation that would ban the rental of video games and computer game software.[44]

Nintendo has also filed patent infringement suits against Magnavox and Atari.[45] While Nintendo's suits may or may not be justified, it is clear that as a company it intends to maintain its domination in the video game market. Yet while doing so, Nintendo is also acutely concerned about diversifying into other areas of media and communications.

Plans are in the works at Nintendo to unveil by 1991 an interactive video game and information system network for the United States. Under the proposed plan, Nintendo Entertainment System video games would function as terminals that would allow long-distance game playing as well as access to financial and news information services. The project will probably be conducted in collaboration with American Telephone and Telegraph (AT&T).[46]

The proposed network is modeled after one that is already available in Japan. Nintendo is confident that AT&T will eventually cooperate in the joint venture. According to Nintendo CEO and President Hiroshi Yamauchi: "AT&T is quite rational and ultimately will cooperate."[47] Nintendo has no intention of remaining just a video game company—its purpose is nothing less than to establish itself as a global electronic communications giant. As Yamauchi explains: "We learned our lessons well from Atari. We are able to understand very clearly why Atari failed. No toy company ever became a big company successfully by remaining a toy company."[48] Nintendo's plan to enter into new markets and to establish itself as a force in communications is made plausible by its extraordinary success in recent years and by the financial capital at its command. It is worth noting, for example, that Microsoft Incorporated of Redmond, Washington, the largest of America's microcomputer software manufacturers, had total sales of approximately $800 million in 1989, while Nintendo showed gross sale figures that were more than twice as large.

## Future Competition for Nintendo

At the present time Turbo-Grafx from NEC and Genesis from Sega ($150 to $200 in most toy stores) have introduced video game players that are clearly superior, from a technological point of view, to Nintendo. By using more powerful 16-bit processing, they offer much sharper graphics and more realistic game action.[49] In the case of the NEC Turbo-Grafx system, an add-on video disk player expands the graphic possibilities for the games far beyond anything that currently exists on the market. In light of these innovations, it seems highly likely that Nintendo will develop game machines and controllers as well as games adapted to the 16-bit chip technology.

One of the interesting potential outgrowths of the introduction of more sophisticated machines into the home video game market is that a hardware base will be established that will make it possible for new types of computer products to be introduced on a mass-market basis. Video disk computer action games will probably lead to the development of interactive simulations for the mass market. These disks have enormous memory and startling graphic capabilities, and it should only be a short while before video rental stores will be marketing video game laser disks based on exploring historical sites, playing video football or baseball, games involving simulated sex, and so on. The distinctions made between video games, video movies, and motion pictures will become increasingly less well defined.

Companies such as Nintendo, acutely aware of the enormous profits available with this new generation of computer games and simulations and of the potential to expand into the adult market, will undoubtedly vigorously pursue new markets. In this context, it is important to reflect on the fact that the world of Nintendo is not simply involved in manufacturing video game players and controllers but is interconnected with larger media and communication systems which have an enormous potential to shape and define our culture.

# 2

# Video Games as Microworlds

Almost thirty years ago Marshall McLuhan wrote in his book *Understanding Media* that "the medium is the message. This is merely to say that the personal and social consequences of any medium—that is, of any extension of ourselves—result from the new scale that is introduced into our affairs by each extension of ourselves, or by any new technology."[1] It has become fashionable in academic circles to dismiss McLuhan and his work as being dated and overly simplistic. And yet as we advance further into the microcomputer revolution, I find myself coming back to many of his ideas. In the context of this book, McLuhan's comments about games and their function in the media are particularly helpful. According to McLuhan:

> Games are popular art, collective, social *reactions* to the main drive or action of any culture. Games, like institutions, are extensions of social man and of the body politic, as technologies are extensions of the animal organism. Both games and technologies are counter-irritants or ways of adjusting to the

stress of the specialized actions that occur in any social group. As extensions of the popular response to the workaday stress, games become faithful models of a culture. They incorporate both the action and the reaction of whole populations in a single dynamic image.[2]

In the movie *The Wizard,* the Nintendo games become overarching symbols for the quest for self that Jimmy has undertaken. Jimmy's confrontation with the unexpected, in particular the new *Mario Bros. 3* game that was thrust on him at the Video Armageddon competition, is no different from the unexpected events that constantly confront one as part of living. In this context, McLuhan argued that "Games are dramatic models of our psychological lives providing release of particular tensions. They are collective and popular art forms with strict conventions. Ancient and nonliterate societies naturally regarded games as live dramatic models of the outer cosmic drama."[3] For Jimmy in his search for self, the symbolic video games that he plays are as real an experience, and as much a part of his becoming whole, as the journey he undertakes with Corey and Haley to Los Angeles.

Turning to a game with mythic overtones, or to literature, in search of meaning in one's life is not a new idea. In his book *The Uses of Enchantment: The Meaning and Importance of Fairy Tales,* Bruno Bettelheim argued that "if we hope to live not just from moment to moment, but in true consciousness of our existence, then our greatest need and most difficult achievement is to find meaning in our lives."[4] Wisdom, according to Bettelheim, does not burst forth fully matured like Athena out of the head of Zeus.

Instead it is acquired gradually, one small step at a time.[5]

For Bettelheim important meaning has been found in our culture in the traditional fairy tale. Quoting Schiller, Bettelheim has argued that "deeper meaning resides in the fairy tales told to me in my childhood than in the truth that is taught to me by life."[6] Bettelheim was convinced that "fairy tales carry important messages to the conscious, the preconscious, and the unconscious mind, on whatever level each is functioning at the time. By dealing with universal human problems, particularly those which preoccupy the child's mind, these stories speak to the budding ego and encourage its development, while at the same time relieving preconscious and unconscious pressures."[7] Bettelheim objected strongly to children's literature that adds little or nothing of importance to one's life. Reading for him has the potential to be an enriching experience—one that is capable of empowering the child. Poorly written children's stories, unlike the great fairy tales of Perrault and the Grimm brothers, cheat the child of the experience of literature—an experience that provides deeper meaning in light of his or her stage of development.

For McLuhan, games can function in much the same way as the fairy tale does for Bettelheim—as a way of bringing meaning to life. According to him, "Games are a sort of artificial paradise like Disneyland, or some Utopian vision by which we interpret and complete the meaning of our daily lives. In games we devise means of nonspecialized participation in the larger drama of our time."[8] But what if the games that we play are corrupt? What if, instead of ennobling the individual, as great literature does, our games debase our humanity? What if our games cheat our children in their quest for deeper meaning? What if they blind the child's vision rather than liberating her consciousness? These are the questions that must be asked in the end as one carefully looks at the culture of video games and more specifically at the world of Nintendo.

## Growth of the Electronic Environment

Since the early 1950s, the youth population in America has become increasingly surrounded by an electronic environment. In the case of television, for example, the average child from the age of six to eighteen will have viewed approximately 16,000 hours of television and spent an additional 4,000 hours listening to radio and records or watching movies. More time will be spent with these media than in school or in talking with parents.[9] Children today are presented with an extraordinarily wide range of electronic media options—ones that are constantly expanding and growing. In addition to commercial television, other options are cable television, video rentals, "Walkman" radios, tape recorders, personal computers, and arcade and home video games.[10]

The growth in the involvement of the youth population in electronic media is revealed by a number of statistics. For example, data collected by Comstock in 1976 indicated that the average sixth grader watched 3.1 hours of television each school day versus 2.8 hours per day in 1967. By 1983, Ellis reported that the daily television viewing of this group had increased to an average of 4.7 hours per day.[11] This represents approximately a 70 percent increase in less than two decades. At the same time that this increase in television viewing has taken place, video games and personal computers have been introduced. In a survey of video games used by sixth graders in Oklahoma, Ellis found that 73 percent of the males and females reported owning a video game and an additional 17 percent a personal computer. In the sample surveyed, the average amount of time spent playing video games was two hours per day. More than half of the boys (52 percent) played games at a video arcade at least once a week, while 38 percent of the girls played at the arcade once a week. Almost half the youths spent $4.00 or more on these outings.[12]

Video games represent a new and important component in the contemporary media scene. As a result, significant questions must be raised. One of the most important is, what is the nature of the environment that the child discovers in the world of video games? In answering this question, one must recognize that first and foremost video games are a symbolic system. Certainly this is nothing new; television likewise presents its viewers with a symbolic system. But, as Ellis explains, on other dimensions video games are fundamentally different from television:

> In video games, symbols of balls with large mouth(s) eat symbols of ghosts; symbols of spacecraft attack symbols of alien invaders; symbols of King Kong drop barrels down on symbols of heroes (themselves symbols of the individuals playing the game) who rescue symbols of maidens (who are symbols of Fay

Wray). All of these marvels, of course, are animated by programs consisting of hundreds of lines of symbols written in computer languages that feature symbols such as "GOTO," "HIRES," and D$ = CHR$(4); INPUT D$.[13]

In this context, the educational theorist C. A. Bowers maintains that computers in general (video games of course being included) are radically redefining patterns of communication, the organization and structure of knowledge, the way in which we interact with the physical world, what we preserve historically, and how we encode the vocabularies of our culture.[14] One of the things I hope to demonstrate in this book is that from a social and cultural point of view, video games are neither a neutral nor a trivial technology. Instead, like other media, they represent important intellectual and social systems that are redefining the symbolic underpinnings of our culture.[15]

## How Video Games Function

In order to begin to understand a phenomenon such as video games, and Nintendo in particular, it is necessary to ask how they function. To begin with, most video games are not educational, only goal-oriented: Mario rescues the Princess and Pac-Man gobbles the dots. The goals pursued and achieved have no particular significance prior to the invention of the game. They are not necessarily connected to a larger culture. And, although they may reflect certain values and beliefs, they are not necessarily goals that are consciously admired or pursued by any particular group in the culture.[16] One would be hard-pressed to find anyone in our society who would value the ability to achieve a maximum number of "head butts"—a goal that is pursued in the game *Double Dragon*.

A second point is that most computer games are internally reinforcing. This is particularly interesting in light of the fact that the games are pointless relative to most educational, social, and cultural needs.[17] One does not become a professional video game player.

A third feature is that video games are extremely fast and complex. Thus it is possible for these games to operate at a rate and level of complexity that differ significantly from the traditional world of mechanical games such as billiards or pool.[18]

A fourth distinction is that the instructions for most video games are written into the game programs. Video games are literally teaching machines that instruct the player using them in the rules of a game as it is being played.[19] The extent to which this is the case is clear in Sherry Turkle's observation that "working out your game strategy involves a process of deciphering the logic of the game, of understanding the intent of the game's designer, of achieving a 'meeting of the minds' with the program. The video games reflect the computer within— in their animated graphics, in the rhythm they impose, in the kind of strategic thinking that they require."[20]

According to Turkle, the computational specificity of computer games becomes particularly clear when they are compared with their "grandparent," pinball. On the surface, pinball and computer games are relatively similar. You stand in front of both games and try to manipulate an object as part of a game scenario or scheme that allows you to accumulate points. Skill is an important part of both types of games. Well-designed games are highly challenging and are rarely totally mastered. Computer games and pinball machines, however, are based on entirely different technologies—one digital and electronic and the other analog and mechanical.[21]

Digital systems such as computer video games "recreate" an object or thing from a binary code; each version is virtually identical. Analog systems such as pinball games create a physical model or approximation. Although similar—that is, analogous—no two versions in analog systems are exactly alike. Thus each pinball machine, because of slight differences in its construction, is likely to have a character and meaning uniquely its own. By comparison, a computer game is virtually the same in every version.

The differences between the assumptions and technologies of each game are profound. Turkle argues that the video game is liberated from the mechanical limitations of the pinball machine.[22] This points to a fifth and final distinction concerning how video games function and operate: they do not necessarily operate within the known physical laws of the universe.[23] Mario can jump enormous heights and crush opponents with his weight and yet suffer no harm to himself. As a result of the use of a digital/electronic means of encoding information, the world of the video game is freed from the constraints of an analog/mechanical universe: "Objects fly, spin, accelerate, change shape and color, disappear and reappear. Their behavior, like the behavior of anything created by a computer program, is limited only by the programmer's imagination. The objects in a video game are representations of objects. And a representation of a ball, unlike a real one, never need obey the laws of gravity unless its programmer wants it to."[24] Pinball games, on the other hand, are part of a physical and mechanically constrained universe. As a child interviewed by Turkle explained, pinball "is fun but it belongs to the real world . . . it's always the same."[25]

Pinball games almost never increase in difficulty; the first ball you play is no more difficult than the last ball. In contrast, computer games can be programmed to contain increasing levels of difficulty. Expert and often highly esoteric knowledge is essential in advancing to the highest levels of a video game. Such specialized knowledge is not a significant part of games such as pinball. Based in the physical and analog world rather than the digital world of the computer, pinball is much more variable. As in dealing with real human beings, there is the requirement of getting to know the machine, with its individual characteristics and quirks. In contrast, computer games are constant and unvarying.

## The Holding Power of Computer Games

Sherry Turkle in *The Second Self* describes watching a thirteen-year-old girl play the computer game *Asteroids* in a small café in New York City's Little Italy. Seemingly possessed by the game, swearing loudly and verbally abusing the owner of the restaurant, she maneuvers her spacecraft through a storm of asteroids and maintains such a violent and rapid firing sequence on the "missile" button that when she concludes the game she complains that her fingers hurt. According to Turkle, "For the girl in the café, mastery of her game was urgent and tense. There is a sense of a force at work, a 'holding power' whose roots are aggressive, passionate, and eroticized."[26]

Such scenes are common. There are a number of explanations for why video games have such extraordinary holding power on those who play them. To begin with, the computational power of the video game makes it possible for scores to have virtually no upper limit. The universe that is defined, although very narrow in its scope, stretches on endlessly. Skill in and of itself is not enough; only expert knowledge provided by the makers of the machines or those involved in the deepest level of analyzing them makes it possible to achieve the higher levels of the game. Turkle points out that video games draw on the machine's ability to support "a simulated world and meditative environment," which resonates with the child's belief that computer toys are "metaphysical machines." Through them the player is promised the possibility of a game that never stops and the possibility of perfection—perhaps even immortality.[27]

Other factors that undoubtedly draw people to video games include the fact that they provide a setting in which individuals can take a series of risks with few negative consequences attached. In addition, video games provide an arena in which skill is the ultimate judge of competence. Thus a small child can potentially compete against an older and stronger adversary.

According to Turkle, the holding power of video

games is closely related to the holding power of computers in general. As she explains:

> Video games are a window onto a new kind of intimacy with machines that is characteristic of the nascent computer culture. The special relationship that players form with video games has elements that are common to interactions with other kinds of computers. The holding power of video games, their almost hypnotic fascination, is computer holding power. The experiences of video game players help us to understand this holding power and something else as well. At the heart of the computer culture is the idea of constructed, "rule-governed" worlds.[28]

As a type of computer, video games create a culture of rules and simulations.[29] In doing so, they represent microworlds complete unto themselves. The images they present are easy to fall in love with, often narcissistic in nature, allowing the player the potential to function within a self-selected and artificial microworld: "Like Narcissus and his reflection, people who work with computers can easily fall in love with the worlds they have constructed or with their performances in the worlds created for them by others. Involvement with simulated worlds affects relationships with the real one."[30]

## What Makes Computer Games Fun?

Over a decade ago Thomas Malone conducted a series of studies to determine why computer games are so captivating.[31] Malone was interested not only in understanding the holding power of computer games, but also in seeing if similar principles could be employed to make learning with computers more interesting and enjoyable.[32]

Malone's initial research involved a survey in which he interviewed sixty-five students from kindergarten through the eighth grade about their preferences in computer games. The children had all been playing computer games for at least two months as part of a weekly computer class. The teachers for the class provided Malone with a list of the twenty-five games that they felt were the most popular among the students. Using this list, he proceeded to ask each child to rate on a three-point scale how much he or she liked a particular game.[33] Table 2.1 lists the twenty-five computer games and the ratings they received from the students in Malone's study.

Malone discovered that the single most important reason for a game's popularity had to do with whether it had a specific goal. In the case of the three most popular games reported to him by the students whom he interviewed, Malone found that each had an obvious goal (*Petball,* getting a high score; *Snake2,* trapping the other person's snake; *Breakout,* destroying all of the bricks). Scoring, audio effects, randomness of the game, speed of answers, visual effects, and competition were also strongly correlated with the game preferences of the students interviewed.[34]

Based on his findings, Malone argued that specific game elements should be incorporated into instructional environments, including (1) challenge, (2) fantasy, and (3) curiosity (Table 2.2). In reviewing his conclusions on what makes an educational program enjoyable, one finds that the basic characteristics of many of the most popular Nintendo games correspond to the suggested criteria he has outlined. In the following section I examine his

*Table 2.1*  Twenty-five computer games listed
according to preference

| Game | Average rating | Description |
|------|---------|-------------|
| *Petball* | 2.8 | Simulated pinball with sound |
| *Snake2* | 2.6 | Two players control motion and shooting of snakes |
| *Breakout* | 2.6 | Player controls paddle to hit ball that breaks through a wall, piece by piece |
| *Dungeon* | 2.6 | Player explores a cave, like Dungeons and Dragons |
| *Chase S* | 2.6 | Two players chase each other across an obstacle course, with sound effects |
| *Star Trek* | 2.5 | Navigate through space and shoot Klingon ships |
| *Don't Fall* | 2.5 | Guess words like Hangman, but instead of a person being hung, a person or robot advances to cliff |
| *Panther* | 2.4 | Guess who committed a murder by questioning witnesses who may lie |
| *Mission* | 2.4 | Bomb submarines without getting your ship sunk |
| *Chaser* | 2.4 | Capture a moving square with perpendicular lines |
| *Chase* | 2.4 | Like Chase S but without sound |
| *Horses* | 2.3 | Bet on horses that race along a track |

*Table 2.1*   (continued)

| Game | Average rating | Description |
|------|----------------|-------------|
| *Sink Ship* | 2.3 | Bomb a ship from an airplane |
| *Snake* | 2.3 | Like Snake2 but snakes can't shoot |
| *Lemonade* | 2.3 | Run a lemonade stand: buy supplies, advertise, etc. |
| *Escape* | 2.2 | Escape from moving robots |
| *Star Wars* | 2.2 | Shoot Darth Vader's ship on screen |
| *Maze Craze* | 2.2 | Escape from randomly generated maze |
| *Hangman* | 2.1 | Guess letters of a word before man is hung |
| *Adventure* | 2.0 | Explore cave with dragons, etc. |
| *Draw* | 2.0 | Make any design on the screen |
| *Stars* | 2.0 | Guess a number; clues given by number of stars |
| *Snoopy* | 1.9 | Shoot Red Baron by subtracting Snoopy's position on number line from Red Baron's position |
| *Eliza* | 1.8 | Converse with simulated psychiatrist |
| *Gold* | 1.5 | Fill in blanks in story about Goldilocks |

*Note:* Sixty-five students were asked to rate the games (1 = don't like; 2 = like, 3 = like a lot).

*Source:* T. W. Malone, "What Makes Computer Games Fun?" BYTE, December 1981, p. 260. © McGraw-Hill, Inc.

*Table 2.2*  Checklist for designing enjoyable
           educational programs

CHALLENGE

*Goal*
• Does the activity have a clear goal? If not, is it easy for the
  students to determine goals of appropriate difficulty for
  themselves?
• Are the goals personally meaningful?

*Uncertain Outcome*
• Does the program have a variable difficulty level?
    • Determined by the student
    • Determined automatically, depending on the student's
      skill
• Does the activity have multiple goal levels?
    • Scorekeeping
    • Speeded responses
• Does the program include randomness?
• Does the program include hidden information selectively
  revealed?

*Fantasy*
• Does the program include an emotionally appealing fantasy?
• Is the fantasy intrinsically related to the skill learned in the
  activity?
• Does the fantasy provide a useful metaphor?

*Curiosity*
Sensory curiosity: audio and visual effects
    • as decoration
    • to enhance fantasy
    • as a reward
    • as a representation system
Cognitive curiosity
    • Does the program include surprises?
    • Does the program include constructive feedback?

*Source:* T. W. Malone, "What Makes Computer Games Fun?" BYTE,
December 1981, p. 266. © McGraw-Hill, Inc.

model in more detail by undertaking a systematic analysis of perhaps the most popular of all of the Nintendo video games, *Super Mario Bros. 2*.

## The Appeal of *Super Mario Bros. 2*

*Super Mario Bros. 2* fits virtually all of the criteria outlined by Malone for defining an enjoyable instructional environment. As described in *Nintendo Power's* review article of the game:

> It started late one night when our hero, Mario, had a very strange dream. In his dream, he climbed up a long winding stairway leading to a door. When he opened the door, he saw a world unlike anything he had ever seen before. As he peered into this wondrous world, he suddenly heard someone say in a faint and distant voice, "Welcome to the World of Dreams, the land of Sub-con. We have been waiting for you, Mario. We want you and your friends to fight against the evil ruler Wart, and bring peace back to the World of Dreams." [35]

*Does the activity have a clear goal?* With the introduction quoted above, the player is immediately faced with a challenge, to "bring peace back to the World of Dreams." This addresses what Malone considers to be the greatest appeal provided by video games—whether or not the game has a clear goal.

Before the game begins, each player is given the option of choosing one of four characters: Mario, Luigi, Toad, or the Princess. In the case of Mario, "his ability to jump is average, but he loses it a little bit when he carries an item." [36] Luigi "can spring up higher, but he greatly weakens if he has to carry an item." [37] Toad "is the worst jumper, but the weight of items does not hinder him one bit."[38] Princess "can float in the air for about 1.5 seconds if you hold down the A button."[39]

*Does the program have a variable difficulty level? Are the goals personally meaningful?* By choosing which character he wants to be, the player is provided with variability in terms of how difficult the game will be to play. Thus the goal is made more personally meaningful because the player has some (although limited) choice over which character he will be in the game. Since each of the characters included in the game has different powers, playing the game the same way with each character will result in very different outcomes.

*Does the program have multiple goal levels?* Multiple goal levels are achieved by the fact that there are seven worlds through which the player advances. Each world has three areas, except for the seventh. All areas include a "Little Boss" who must be defeated. Each of the worlds and areas has different challenges and demands that the player use different skills to overcome the "Little Boss." Score-keeping is provided automatically as the player advances through different levels and at the same time acquires increased power and "lives."

Accelerated responses are possible through the individual player's use of his or her control system and the use of instruments or vehicles found within the game. A "Flying Carpet," for example, appears in Area 2 of World 1; with it the player is able to negotiate his way through the area much more easily than would otherwise be possible.

*Does the program include randomness?* Randomness is provided in the game as a result of the player making different choices, which in turn creates different scenarios for moving on to the various goals. In this context, it is worth noting that despite the seeming randomness provided by this aspect of the game's design, the scenarios are not totally unfamiliar and can be reasonably controlled by the player.

*Does the program include hidden information selectively revealed?* As the player works his or her way through the dangers of the World of Dreams, various items are revealed that help one cope with one's enemies: "Some of them help you get the best of your enemies. Others are very handy for restoring your character's life or moving the characters to more advantageous places. The appearance of items might change in each world, but the effectiveness is just the same."[40] Examples of items that are revealed or discovered by the players that empower the players' characters include "Sprout," "Stopwatch," "Cherries," "Star Man," "1-Up," "Vegetables," "Mushroom Block," "Mushroom," "Potion," "Shells," "Key," "Bomb," "Heart," "Pow," "Coin," and "Rocket." The Rocket, for example, which is capable of taking a player's character to different places, appears when the character pulls up grass at certain spots.[41]

Interestingly, expert knowledge is selectively revealed to players outside of the actual game through sources such as the Nintendo Information Hotline, peer group exchanges, and articles in magazines such as *Nintendo Power*. A review article of *Super Mario Bros. 2* published in *Nintendo Power* magazine, for example, explains how to destroy the character Birdo, who is the area's "Little Boss" in Area 1 of World 1: "The first Little Boss is Birdo. He sometimes, but not always, spits eggs to attack you. When you have a chance, hop on top of the flying egg. Pick up the flying egg by quickly pressing "B." Aim and throw the eggs back at Birdo. If you hit him three times, he'll go down." [42]

*Does the program include an emotionally appealing fantasy?* The fantasy built into the game is emotionally appealing in that the player's characters (and thus the player) are enlisted to "fight against the evil ruler Wart, and bring peace back to the World of Dreams." [43]

*Is the fantasy intrinsically related to the skill learned in the activity?* Mario and the other characters in the game learn to use secret potions, to throw bombs, and to read carefully the terrain of the World of Dreams in order to be able to overcome and defeat the "Little Bosses" such as Ostro, Beezo, Birdo, Autobomb, Ninji, and Phanto, and ultimately the "Big Boss," Wart. Wart is "the most mischievous of all of the rascals in the World of Dreams" who created the other monsters in the World of Dreams by playing with the Dream Machine. [44]

*Does the fantasy provide a useful metaphor?* The fantasy in *Super Mario Bros. 2* provides the metaphor of good engaged in a struggle to overcome evil, as basic and fundamental an archetype as is likely to be found in human culture (God versus the devil in *Paradise Lost;* Darth Vader versus Luke Skywalker in *Star Wars;* and so forth).

*Sensory curiosity as decoration, to enhance fantasy, as a reward, and as a representation system.* The game is built around fast action and highly colorful graphics, with a catchy if repetitive musical accompaniment.

*Does the program include surprises?* The game is filled with surprises, ranging from evil bosses with different personalities and characteristics to magic potions and keys.[45]

*Does the program include constructive feedback?* Constructive feedback is provided to a player by means of her character's power being increased or decreased by gaining or losing "lives" and by making it through the various levels of the game to the final confrontation with Wart.

What is the significance of all this? In his book *Mindstorms,* Seymour Papert describes how children using the computer language LOGO are in fact "learning how to exercise control over an exceptionally rich and sophisticated 'micro world.'"[46] *Super Mario Bros. 2* and other video games like it are also microworlds. The reason they are so compelling is that they systematically tap into children's needs for fantasy and imagination.

In addition, video games provide a means by which the player can control an electronic environment. In this case, analogies to reading and writing are useful. One can read the written word and in turn shape the written word by writing oneself. Similarly, one can watch an electronic medium related to television, a video game, and in turn shape it by playing it. As Patricia Greenfield has commented: "It is possible that, before the advent of video games, a generation brought up on film and television was in a bind: the most active medium of expression, writing, lacked the quality of visual dynamism. Television had dynamism, but could not be affected by the viewer. Video games are the first medium to combine visual dynamism with an active participatory role for the child."[47] Video games like *Super Mario Bros. 2* may in fact be the means by which their users step into a new type of electronic dialogue and, in turn, literacy. As I will demonstrate in subsequent chapters, the issue to be confronted is whether the options of exercising literacy are highly circumscribed because of the nature of the computer that runs the system or because of the content of its programming. A child picking up a pencil and applying it to paper can potentially create an infinitely rich microworld—one limited only by the constraints of her imagination. In the electronic environment of video games—at least as they are currently designed and function—the possibilities of the microworlds that can be created are much more limited. In the case of the computer (and by extension, the video game), tremendous flexibility and the potential for exploration and self-definition can be built into any system. This is not the case with Nintendo.

In preliminary interviews for this book, I asked a group of eight- and nine-year-old boys what they would like most if they could design a video game best suited to their needs. In response, they talked about wanting to be able to define the characters in their game, to shape the power that they had, and to design the settings in which the games took place. Such desires suggest that children are trapped in microworlds created by computer programmers, which, although highly appealing, are ultimately limited in terms of the needs and interests of the children who play the games.

# 3

# Research on Video Games

With the proliferation of video games in both arcade and home settings in the past decade, there has been widespread speculation about their potential negative effect on the children and adolescents who play them. Despite this concern, relatively little substantive analysis of the games has been undertaken. In this chapter, through a review of the existing literature in the field, I attempt to address the question of the sociological and psychological implications of video games. Since the early 1980s, a research literature has begun to emerge that can provide insight into this and related questions. Because the field is so new, most of the literature written up to this time deals with arcade games rather than home video games. Many of the conclusions drawn from studies on arcade video games, however, can be directly applied to home video game systems such as Nintendo. It should be noted that most of these studies were done from a psychological perspective— a fact that tends to emphasize certain aspects of video game use while ignoring or de-emphasizing other important questions that need to be taken into account.

## Reactions to Video Games and Their Content

Many people respond to video games on a largely emotional level. In late 1982, for example, the U.S. Surgeon General, C. Everett Koop, warned that video games were producing "aberrations in childhood behavior." According to him, children were becoming addicted to the games "body and soul." Yet when asked to substantiate his comments, Koop admitted that he had no scientific evidence to support his point of view.[1]

Koop's criticisms of video games have been echoed by other professionals, as well as the general public. The social psychologist Philip Zimbardo, for example, has commented: "Eat him, burn him, zap him is the message rather than bargaining and cooperation. Most games tend to feed into masculine fantasies of control, power and destruction."[2] Some local communities have banned video game arcades, arguing that they encourage aggressive behavior in children and create an unwholesome environment.[3] In the Philippines, video games have been described as being "a destructive social bandit." Sentiment against the games became so strong that in November 1981, then-President Ferdinand Marcos declared a nationwide ban on the machines, giving their owners two weeks to destroy them.[4]

Concern about the games is in fact justified. One need only visit a local video game arcade to realize the extent to which violence is overwhelmingly emphasized in most video game scenarios. Games such as *Double Dragon* and *Bad Dudes*—among the most popular of all arcade games in recent years—are both based on martial arts themes. Savage kicks and the ability to use violent weapons against one's opponents are what determine success in the games. Other arcade game scenarios include alien invasions (*Galaga* and *Contra*), prize fighting (*Punch-Out*), and guerrilla warfare (*Guerrilla*).

Violence dominates not only the video games found in the arcades but also those included on home game systems such as Nintendo, many of which were first introduced in video arcade settings. *Bionic Commando,* which was ranked as the twelfth most popular game in a November 1989 player's poll by *Nintendo Power* magazine,[5] is described in the *Game Player's Buyer's Guide to Nintendo Games* as having a scenario in which

> Top secret agent Super Joe has been captured behind enemy lines. You've been sent to rescue him. It's a tough mission, but you've got a tough weapon—a mechanical grappling device known as a bionic arm. Swing from building to building and level to level, or use the arm as a weapon to mow down anyone who gets in the way. Great fun, great action . . . a great adventure.[6]

*Rampage,* which ranks twenty-third in popularity in the *Nintendo Power* player's poll, is described in the same issue of the *Buyer's Guide* as being a game in which one needs to

> Eat your fill—the entire city is at your feet. Literally. Pick a monster and attack as many U.S. cities as you can stomach. Smash the buildings, eat the

people, and wreck any of the helicopters, tanks, or cars that get in your way. Search the buildings for cheeseburgers, and other goodies. But watch out for poison and electrical appliances. When a big guy like you gets indigestion, *everyone* suffers.[7]

*P.O.W. (Prisoners of War),* which was first developed as an arcade game and then reintroduced on the Nintendo system, is typical of many of the games. An advertisement for the game explains how the player is

> Surrounded . . . Captured . . . Imprisoned in an enemy war camp! You'll have to fight your way to freedom with your bare fists. But if you can break into the ammunition depot, you'll find grenades, knives, and M-16's to tilt the odds in your favor. This is the prison camp they call "escape-proof." But they've never had to reckon with this P.O.W.![8]

As I will explore in more detail in Chapter 6, the world of Nintendo—and video games in general—is one of violence and mayhem populated by prize fighters, terrorists, S.W.A.T. teams, Ninja warriors, robotic cops, bad dudes, and adolescent mutant turtles.

In addition to reflecting themes of violence and destruction, video games have a history of being sexist and racist. In the early 1980s the home video game *Custer's Revenge* had to be withdrawn from circulation as a result of consumer protests over its discriminatory treatment of women and Native Americans. Players who were able to maneuver Custer through thorny cactus and a hail of arrows got to watch an officer sexually assault a helpless but smiling Indian woman tied to a stake. Another game from the period, *Communist Mutants from Space,* had swarms of Marxists from the planet Rooskie attack the earth. These Communist mutants, hatched from a mother creature and filled with irradiated vodka, tried to enslave the planet. The object of the game was to have the player save the planet, keeping it free for democracy and the free enterprise system.[9]

## Video Games and Social Behavior

How does video game playing affect the general social interaction and behavior of children? Are children who play video games significantly influenced by their content? In an attempt to address these questions, a limited body of research has been undertaken in order to examine the impact of the games on their users.

In terms of social interaction, Gibb and his colleagues discovered in a key 1983 study of 280 video game players that on personality dimensions of self-esteem/self-degradation, social deviance/social conformity, hostility/kindness, social withdrawal/gregariousness, obsessiveness and compulsiveness, and achievement motivation, there was no significant relationship between these measures and the amount of time people spent playing video games.[10]

In a 1983 study based on a large survey of video game players in Los Angeles, Brooks concluded that video game playing was to some extent a social activity and not as "addictive" or "compulsive" as it might at first appear. Most youths spent less than half of the time they were in an arcade actually playing games; the rest of the time was spent talking to friends and engaging in other social activities.[11] In a related study, Egli and Meyers interviewed 151 males and females in three video game arcades in Sacramento, California, and came to similar conclusions. Identifying approximately 10 percent of their subjects as eliciting some sort of compulsive behavior in the amount of time they devoted to playing video games, they concluded that in most instances video games played a relatively minor part in the lives of their subjects, and that little support could be found for the idea that video game playing reduced participation in active sports or was related to poor school performance.[12]

Edna Mitchell in a qualitative study of family interaction and video games concluded that the games "brought families together in common recreational interaction more than any other activity in recent memory."[13] While game playing was male-dominated, more than 50 percent of the females included in the study indicated a sense of growing competence and pride in terms of their video game playing.[14]

## Psychoanalytic Theory and Video Games

Attempts to understand the psychodynamics of video games are largely absent from the psychological literature. Martin Klein, in an article in the *Journal of Psychohistory,* raises a number of basic issues in this context. While interesting, his work is largely speculative in nature and perhaps overly dramatic. Among the questions he raises are the following: Are video games somehow different in their psychological impact from pinball, their corollary?

Are the games addictive, and if they are, are they potentially beneficial, neutral, or detrimental to the individual and his or her development? Why is the mesmerizing character of many of the games specific to adolescents? What is the relationship between the content of the video games and the spirit or meaning of the larger culture or society? And finally, what is the meaning of video games and the culture which they create in the context of a psychoanalytic/developmental paradigm?[15]

Klein's interpretations of the games and their meaning are strongly grounded in psychoanalytic theory. According to him, video game "addicts" are

> . . . fallen knights. Due to the primitive group-fantasies of the culture, it appears that these adolescents are insufficiently prepared to contend with their age-appropriate conflicts . . . Unable to withstand the dreadful weight of confusion, these paralyzed adolescents regress to the oral stage of development where the core defense mechanism is withdrawal. With their hand tightly grasping the video game's manual control, the "joy stick," these adolescents enter a richly saturated autoerotic—even autistic— fantasy world that is perfectly designed by their creators to capture the conflicts and struggles of fixated youths.[16]

Klein argues that "the ultimate object of virtually all video games is survival. The video game player is presented with a fantasy environment which he or she is capable of controlling. The intrinsic emphasis on clarity and structure—the player prior to entering the Pac-Man world is clear about the rules pertaining to the exact time, location and reason for each specified action—appears to compensate for the fixated adolescent's untrusting predisposition."[17] Drawing on psychoanalytic theory, Klein argues that video games largely focus around oral sadomasochistic fantasies of the fear of engulfment. This is in turn accompanied by a complementary reaction of aggressive tendencies: "In the space games you shoot them before they shoot you; in Pac-Man you must eat them before they eat you; and in the comic character games you must assault the creature before it assaults you."[18]

The most popular of the early video games was Pac-Man. According to Klein, its popularity was probably due to its

> . . . heavy emphasis on oral symbolism. The themes and strategies of the game perfectly accommodate the adolescent's relation to the world. The Pac-Man creature, which the player controls and symbolically becomes, is all mouth and is referred to as "Jaws." "Jaws" spends his time and energy running from the engulfing monsters. There are four different types of monsters, each with its own personality: "Shadow" always follows you; "Bashful" will run away when you turn around; "Ambition" is always willing to attack you; and "Speedy" is fast and will run over you. Plagued by fear and paranoia, "Jaws" is condemned to eat the fruits of the game while on the run. Its only sanctuary is the tunnel, alias the tube or time warp—the womb—where it can rest apart from the struggles of life. The goal of the game is to eat the magical energizers, which like Popeye's spinach bestows upon "Jaws" the power to undo its misery, turn about, and retaliate by eating the monsters.[19]

In a 1984 study on personality, psychopathology, and developmental issues in video game use, Kestenbaum and Weinstein support many of Klein's assumptions. They argue, for example, that in the case of heavy video game users the games provide

> . . . an arena for modulating the different needs and conflicts which they are experiencing, some of which may be exacerbated by the transition into adolescence. As such, we hypothesize that it plays a homeostatic role in the process of development and adaptation, rather than an inflammatory or pathogenic one. In this regard, video game playing may be an example of a "narcissistic guardian" (Beneson, 1980), which is turned to during periods of developmental stress, and which provides an arena for conflict resolution in fantasy akin to the role of transitional objects in infancy (Busch et al., 1973; Winnicott, 1953) and of imaginary friends in childhood (Nagera, 1969).[20]

Following the arguments of Kestenbaum and Weinstein, it would seem reasonable to assume that video games do not contribute to deviant behavior, but may in fact help adolescents and youths in the developmental process. This conclusion is strongly confirmed by Kestenbaum and Weinstein's survey of nearly 500 junior high school students in an urban and middle-class neighborhood.[21] Experiments comparing the use of biofeedback mechanisms and video games with incarcerated youths conducted by Kappes and Thompson in 1985 also confirm Kestenbaum and Weinstein's conclusions.[22]

If video games provide a release for juveniles and adolescents, and in turn can potentially contribute to their development, then is it logical to assume that the games encourage deviant behavior? In the following section I explore this question in more detail.

## Video Games and Delinquency

Video game arcades, and to a lesser degree home video game systems, provide their users with an alternative social and cultural space. In the past, institutions such as pool halls, soda shops, and pinball arcades have served this function for many youths. In these settings, individuals can meet members of their peer group, institute cultural and social traditions of their own, and relieve boredom and stress. Pool, pinball, or video games allow a means by which to establish hierarchies of skill and ability, and ultimately leadership.[23]

In addition, video games, compared to games such as pinball or pool, provide extremely powerful symbols that can be used to mold a youth subculture. To begin with, there is the aura and mystique of the computer. Video games are high technology. They are the future. The military uses them. They are the basis for space flight and lend themselves to the creation of highly imaginative alternative worlds. In addition, as mentioned earlier, they can be linked to already existing popular cultural systems such as films and sports figures.

Like the pool hall, the video game arcade is generally off limits to parents and adults.[24] For teenagers this means the ability to establish a separate and autonomous culture. This may be achieved in the case of home video games as a result of the fact that the technology is so new and constantly changing that many adults are excluded from it, thus making it a relatively secret and protected domain.

In the Broadway musical *The Music Man,* the introduction of a pool hall into River City is seen as having the potential to thoroughly corrupt the local youth. Similar arguments are made today about video games and more specifically video game arcades. A 1984 study by Ellis, however, suggests that video arcades do little or nothing to encourage deviant behavior in youths. According to Ellis, who surveyed 258 sixth, seventh, and eighth grade working-class children in metropolitan Toronto, on average the subjects in his study spent ten hours watching television, five hours reading, and two playing a team sport per week for every hour spent in a video arcade.[25] Ellis did find small numbers of children who played the games involved in various types of deviant behavior in arcade settings. These children, however, were clearly lacking strong parental supervision and control and were already engaged in undesirable types of social behavior. Hanging out at an arcade could not be causally connected to their deviant behavior.

Kestenbaum and Weinstein suggest that the anxiety about video game playing is largely a parental issue. According to them, the games provide an important adolescent vehicle for fantasy that can help promote growth. Referring in general to adolescent fads that parents have become anxious about in the past and have attempted to control, they suggest that "these parental anxieties and global reactions are often disproportionate to the actual dangers involved, and instead emanate from unresolved parental conflicts and developmental issues, at times dating back to their own childhood."[26]

In summation, video games, and more specifically attendance at video game arcades, probably do not contribute significantly to deviant behavior on the part of children and adolescents. Concern on the part of parents and other members of the adult community may in fact reflect their fear of losing control over youth populations. For this reason, the video game arcade settings where they are frequently found may be made even more attractive to these youths.

## Gender Differences in Video Game Playing

Important differences evidently exist in the ways in which women versus men respond to video games. Most likely these differences can be attributed to social conditioning. Whatever the case, women are demonstrably less attracted to arcade playing, as well as to the social subcultures that have come into existence around games such as Nintendo.

In a 1985 study of college undergraduates by Morlock and colleagues concerning what motivates people to play video games, it was concluded that women prefer more whimsical, less aggressive, and to some degree less demanding games than men. Stimulus characteristics included in the games were found to appeal differently to men and women. Women, for example, were much more interested in the sounds made by the games than were men.[27]

Kiesler, Sproull, and Eccles speculate that women may feel less comfortable than men with the aggressive themes that are emphasized in computer games; that they may have a more difficult time with certain aspects of the spatial and manipulative skills demanded by the games; and that they may not feel comfortable in the arcade atmospheres where the games are often played. In the case of this last point, they believe that when one enters the video arcade, except for "the electronic bells and whistles, you will see the poolroom of yesterday. Like the poolroom, it is largely a male preserve, a place where boys and young men gather."[28] The fact that video game arcades are primarily a male domain is important. According to Kiesler and colleagues, the video arcade provides many children with their first introduction to the culture of computers. The models that are provided tend to exclude women. Video games, for example, are designed by males for other males. Female characters are rarely emphasized as having a leading role in video game scenarios.[29]

The extent to which video games are almost exclusively populated by males can be seen in research by Terri Toles. In a sample of 100 video arcade games, Toles determined that 92 percent of the games did not include any female roles, and that of the remaining 8 percent of the games, 6 percent had females assuming "damsel in distress" roles and 2 percent in active roles. Interestingly, in the case of the two females who do take active roles, neither is human—one being a Mama Kangaroo attempting to retrieve her child and the second a feminized blob, Ms. Pac-Man.[30]

It should not be surprising, therefore, that females do not show the same sort of interest in arcade games as males. Research by Kiesler and colleagues suggests that when girls do go to video arcades they tend to do so as guests, their primary function being to admire the performance of their boyfriends. In an informal survey of a video arcade located in a suburban Pittsburgh shopping mall, Kiesler and colleagues counted 175 players of which only 30 were girls. While girls occasionally played together in groups, the remainder were with boys. No girls were reported as playing the games by themselves.[31]

Males and females may respond to video games differently on the basis of what is demanded of them by the game. Referring to the 1974 work of Maccoby and Jacklin, Kiesler and colleagues point to the fact that boys excel more than girls in visual and spatial tasks that involve depth perception and the solving of mazes or puzzles. The skill of boys versus girls in these areas may be related to cultural training. The fact remains, though, that these types of skills are strongly emphasized in many video games.[32] Talking about computers in general, Kiesler and colleagues in fact argue that there is no particular reason why women should have more difficulty handling computers than men do:

> Computers are not machines in the traditional sense. The essence of computer literacy is really procedural thinking. There is no evidence that girls are deficient in this respect, or that their early training and interests are inconsistent with it. Indeed, computer programming is more like following a recipe or pattern than fixing a bike. If some of the initial alienating elements were removed, girls would be as likely as boys to take the steps toward computer efficacy.[33]

Dan Gutman, a computer journalist, speculates that the success of video arcade games such as *Pac-Man, Q\*Bert, BurgerTime, Domino Man,* and *Millipede* is a direct result of the fact that they are based on "cute, cuddly characters" who are nonviolent and may appeal more to women than men.[34]

# The Relationship between Video Games and Television

An interesting relationship, whose significance is only beginning to be fully appreciated, exists between video game playing and television viewing. Selnow and Reynolds in a 1983 study found that total weekly television viewing was closely related to frequency of attendance at video game arcades and the amount of money spent by individuals on games.[35] In an article by Robinson that presents alternatives to television viewing as either complementary to it or in competition with it, video games were seen as being a complementary type of activity.[36]

In a 1984 study of arcade video game playing, Selnow administered a three-part questionnaire to 244 children between the ages of ten and fourteen attending a statewide summer sports camp.[37] Children who reported that they played video arcade games at least some of the time (83 percent) were asked to complete the third part of the questionnaire. The subjects of the study were then asked to respond to a series of questions on a four-point scale ranging from "always true" to "never true." These questions derived in large part from previous research by Greenberg dealing with the gratification of personal needs received by watching television (as a means of diversion, to learn about things, to pass time, to forget, to learn about oneself, for arousal, for relaxation, for companionship, and as a habit).[38]

A factor analysis of the results by Selnow led him to report the following:

(a) Videogames rate higher than human companions—the games were viewed as more exciting and more fun than human companions; (b) videogames teach about people—they teach about others or serve as surrogates for them; (c) companionship; (d) action—the videogame player has a direct, personal involvement in the action of the game; and (e) solitude/escape. The index of videogame playing was significantly correlated with each of the five factors: videogames preferred to friends ($r = .219$, $p$, .001); learn about people ($r = .148$, $p$, .001; companionship ($r = .267$, $p$, .0010; action ($r = .215$, $p$, .001); solitude/escape ($r = .267$, $p < .001$). Each of these positive correlations provides evidence that heavier videogame players are more likely than less frequent players to perceive that the videogames offer specific gratifications (many of the same gratifications reported in television research).[39]

Selnow discusses the fact that video games may complement television viewing in important ways. Video games allow the viewers to engage themselves actively in the scenarios presented, while television simply provides a vicarious experience: "Given the complementary relationship existing between television viewing and videogame playing, it may be that heavy viewers, so often deprived of active participation and control in their environment with television, are most eager to engage in the comparatively more involving videogames."[40]

Selnow finally comes to the conclusion that adolescents play video games for many of the same reasons they watch television. Through the game medium

> they are temporarily transported from life's problems by their playing, they experience a sense of personal involvement in the action when they work the controls, and they perceive the videogames as not

only a source of companionship, but possibly as a substitute for it. Heavy users of videogames may be "satisficing" their companionship need with videogames rather than with less readily available (less fun, less exciting) human companions.[41]

Arguments such as these fit quite well into McLuhan's argument that games

. . . are contrived and controlled situations, extensions of group awareness that permit a respite from customary patterns. They are a kind of talking to itself on the part of society as a whole. And talking to oneself is a recognized form of play that is indispensable to any growth of self-confidence. The British and Americans have enjoyed during recent times an enormous self-confidence born of the playful spirit of fun and games.[42]

## Video Games and Aggression

Undoubtedly the major area of concern about video games has been whether or not they encourage aggressive behavior in the people who play them. A significant line of research paralleling studies on television and aggression has developed that attempts to address this issue.

In the television research on aggression, two theoretical models have emerged: stimulation theory and catharsis theory. According to stimulation theory, individuals who view violent activities have a greater tendency to commit acts of aggression in real life. In contrast, catharsis theory predicts that observing violence purges the individual of the desire to act aggressively. Although the research is not conclusive, the evidence seems to be in favor of stimulation theory rather than catharsis theory.[43]

Although on the surface the parallels between video game playing and television watching seem obvious, there are important distinctions which need to be taken into account. To begin with, television is a passive medium; viewers have virtually no control over what takes place on the screen. Video games, in contrast, represent an active medium. Television does not require the viewer to pay constant attention to it, whereas video games require total concentration. Finally, television presents actual acts of violence (as in news reports) or detailed simulations of violence (as in detective shows), while video games represent violence at a more abstracted level (space invaders marching in rows across the video screen).

To compare video game violence to television violence is a much more complex issue than may seem to be the case at first. It is important to emphasize that the content of video games, and their technology as well, are rapidly changing. As a result, interpretations of their impact on players based on research drawn largely out of video arcade and home video game studies conducted in the early and mid-1980s may prove to be highly misleading. Joseph Dominick, one of the more useful sources on video games and aggression, argues that: "Videogame violence is abstract and generally consists of blasting spaceships or stylized aliens into smithereens. Rarely does it involve one human being doing violence to another, as is often the case on conventional television. Videogame violence might perhaps be more closely related to abstract violence in some TV cartoons."[44] When Dominick first made this argument in 1984, it may have been valid. It is increasingly questionable now, however. In recent years video games have come to be dominated by martial arts themes, as well as by scenarios focused around international terrorism and extortion. In the game *Thundercade,* for example:

> Terrorism has reached new heights. AATOM (Atomic Age Terrorist Organization of Miracali) has constructed its own nuclear power plant, and threatened the world with atomic terror. The world powers have decided to initiate operation THUNDERCADE to stop AATOM. Equipped with a high-performance combat motorcycle, sidecar cannons, and backed by a precision B-7 bomber, you start out on your dangerous mission.[45]

In *Shinobi,* a popular martial arts game,

> You are Jo Musashi: Master Ninja. Your mission is to rescue the children of the world's leaders from underlings of the feared Ring of Five, a gang of evil terrorist Ninjas. Armed with shruiken, nunchakus, sword, bombs, guns, and your own agility, you must infiltrate their strongholds in order to save the hostages and rid the world of this vile plague.[46]

There is a significant difference between shooting a series of stylized and abstracted spaceships, as is the case in the classic video game *Space Invaders,* and throwing body blocks and head kicks in martial arts games such as *Double Dragon, Bad Dudes,* or *Shinobi.* Whether these games encourage more aggressive behavior in their users needs to be determined by future research.

In addition, the new technology associated with "virtual reality" systems also needs to be carefully studied. With the use of Mattell's Power Glove or Broderbund's U-Force game controller, it has become possible literally to enter into the action of the computer, so that "in *Mike Tyson's Punch Out!!* for example, when you make a fist and throw a left hook, the character on the screen instantly does the same thing."[47] It seems plausible that devices like the Power Glove and U-Force would greatly increase the potential for encouraging children to act aggressively. However, throwing a punch in real life, unlike the Mike Tyson game, does have real consequences: in real life people strike back when hit.

Dominick's 1984 study suggests that playing video games was correlated with aggression, but that when combined with other factors, the video game/ aggression relationship became insignificant.[48] In a 1986 observational study by Cooper and Mackie, it was found that after playing an aggressive video game (*Missile Command*) boys evidenced no increase in aggressive behavior in a free play situation, while girls who had played the same game did evidence increased aggressive behavior. Aggressive behavior also increased on the part of girls when they observed other children playing an aggressive video game. Mackie and Cooper attributed this gender difference to the fact that "girls who are exposed less to violence in general and who are less experienced with violent video games . . . in particular, react to exposure to the aggressive game with greater arousal than boys. This arousal in turn makes aggressive behavior more likely, and so we find more aggressive play in our female subjects than in our male ones."[49]

In a 1986 series of experimental studies conducted with undergraduate students at Rice University, Anderson and Ford concluded that when compared to individuals who had played less aggressive games, those subjects who had played high aggression games were significantly more anxious than those who had played mildly aggressive games or the control group, who had played no game at all.[50]

Silvern and Williamson in a 1987 study of the effects of video game playing on young children concluded that significant increases in aggressive behavior compared to baseline behavior occurred in children between the ages of four and six both after watching violent cartoons and playing the video game *Space Invaders*.[51] Silvern and Williamson's findings confirmed earlier findings of Favaro that any activity—playing video games, television viewing, or dart throwing—when played in aggressive modes increased subjects' subsequent tendencies toward aggressive behavior.[52]

Finally, in a 1985 study by Graybill and colleagues, children who played violent video games tended to manifest more assertive fantasy behavior than children who played nonaggressive games.[53] A subsequent 1987 study by Graybill and others found that the effects of violent versus nonviolent video games on the aggressive behavior of subjects were not significantly different. Graybill and his colleagues attributed the possible differences between the 1985 and 1987 studies to the validity of the dependent measure in the earlier study.[54]

What emerges from the studies on video games and aggressive behavior is that there does seem to be a significant relationship between aggressive behavior on the part of subjects and the playing of video games. What the long-term impact of the games is on aggressive behavior is not known.

It should also be pointed out that a major limitation of this research involves which games were used to elicit aggressive behavior. As pointed out earlier, there is a major difference between a game such as *Space Invaders,* in which rows of alien spaceships descend down a screen and are shot at by the player, and games such as *Bad Dudes* or *Mike Tyson's Punch Out!!* where one engages in hand-to-hand combat or a prize fight. And new technologies such as virtual reality game controllers may also affect levels of aggression manifested by game players.

In summary, results from research conducted up to this time on video games suggest that while the games probably do not contribute significantly to deviant behavior, they do—at least on a short-term basis—increase the aggressive behavior of the individuals who play them. It is also clear that a great deal more research needs to be undertaken before definitive statements can be made about video games and their impact on children and adolescents.

An important starting point is the question of how video games interact with other media such as film and television. This type of investigation will have critical significance as media and games become increasingly integrated in hypermedia formats in the future. McLuhan's recognition that games are media is an extremely important issue to take into account—one that is emphasized even more by the evolution of games into increasingly sophisticated electronic formats.

It should also be emphasized that virtually all of the research conducted on video games has been of a largely psychological nature. The few exceptions to this are research studies conducted by communication theorists or educators. In all this research there has been virtually no work done on the social and cultural content of the games and their potential impact on their users and the culture in general. This is a remarkable oversight, since it is in this domain that the games probably have their greatest potential impact and significance. In the following chapters I will begin to explore this much-neglected and extremely significant area.

# 4

# Play and the Cultural Content of Games

One might be tempted to dismiss the content of video games such as Nintendo as simply a minor aspect of American popular culture—one that has little meaning or significance in the context of the larger society. But as Terri Toles argues, the world of play and games, including Nintendo, "allows for a subtle expression of the ways of perceiving consensual reality held by a culture. Games serve as extensions of social man, giving new meaning to social structures that have become so familiar that their meaning is forgotten or obscured as we conduct the routine activities of everyday life."[1] According to Marshall McLuhan, "games are extensions, not of our private but of our social selves"; they are media of communication—in fact a significant part of the mass media—a series of "situations contrived to permit simultaneous participation of many people in some significant pattern of their own corporate lives."[2]

Ironically, although games are part of the social machinery of our culture, they also allow a means to escape or transcend the day-to-day pressures imposed by the culture. According to McLuhan, games—and this particularly applies to computer games—provide the player with "a release from the monopolistic tyranny of the social machine."[3] For a few brief moments the child can escape the tyranny of school and the social demands of his family and peers by becoming part of an alternate world of galactic invasions, bionic men, teenage mutant Ninja turtles, and damsels in distress who must be rescued. But in entering this world the child must, to a certain degree, surrender his or her freedom. As McLuhan points out:

> A game is a machine that can get into action only if the players consent to become puppets for a time. For individualist Western man, much of his "adjustment" to society has the character of a personal surrender to the collective demands. Our games help both to teach us this kind of adjustment and also to provide a release from it. The uncertainty of the outcomes of our contests makes a rational excuse for the mechanical rigor of the rules and procedures of the game.[4]

Video games represent an extension of the individual or group. Like any medium of information, "its effect on the group or individual is a reconfiguring of the parts of the group or individual that are *not* so extended. A work of art has no existence or function apart from its *effects* on human observers. And art, like games or popular arts, and like media of communication, has the power to impose its own assumptions by setting the human community into new relationships and postures."[5]

The potential of games—and more specifically

video games—to impose their own assumptions by shifting the human community into new relationships and postures is an issue that has been inadequately addressed in the context of video games in general, and of Nintendo in particular. Through a careful examination of the social and cultural content of games included in the Nintendo system, we can begin to glean insights into the psychological and social forms that characterize our society. As Toles points out: "Games in human development may provide a bridge between child-training pressures and adult cultural forms . . . Games may offer a buffered experience of fortune (through games of chance), achievement (games of physical skills) or leadership (games of strategy). Games are also exercises in mastery by the player of the relevant social stratum in which she operates."[6] In this chapter I examine in detail the social and cultural content of games that are available as part of the world of Nintendo, with the assumption that computer games are "cultural texts whose meanings are amenable to interpretation."[7]

## Computers and the Selection and Amplification of Culture

In his work *The Cultural Dimensions of Educational Computing: Understanding the Non-Neutrality of Technology,* C. A. Bowers questions at the most basic level whether the technology of the computer and its use in education are neutral. According to him, "the most fundamental question about the new technology has never been seriously raised by either the vocal advocates or the teachers who have attempted to articulate their reservations. The question has to do with whether the technology is neutral; that is, neutral in terms of accurately representing, at the level of the software program, the domains of the real world in which people live."[8] Bowers argues that the failure to recognize this question is liable to continue as long as educators and the more general public fail to recognize that microcomputers and the software that accompanies them are "part of the much more complex symbolic world that makes up our culture."[9]

Drawing on the work of the sociologist Erving Goffman, Bowers argues that we need to reframe how we look at computers and the way in which they function: instead of simply looking at computers in a technical and procedural context, we need to deal with them in a larger cultural context. Furthermore, we need to recognize that computers and the software that is written for them mediate the student or the child's understanding of his culture.[10]

Following Bowers's model of educational computing, we can look at video games as being instrumentalities through which the child's understanding of his culture is mediated. In this context, video games such as Nintendo are neither neutral nor harmless, but represent very specific social and symbolic constructs. In effect, the games become powerful teaching machines and instruments of cultural transmission.

Computers mediate cultural constructs through both the hardware and more specifically the software on which they are based. Drawing on the ideas of Don Ihde as outlined in his book *Technics and Praxis,* Bowers points to the importance of asking what it is that the computer selects for *amplification* and what it selects for *reduction*.[11] The same question applies to video games, and more specifically to Nintendo. In the research literature on video games, as discussed in the previous chapter, questions such as those raised by Bowers in the context of educational computing are almost totally ignored. In large part this can be explained by the fact that most of the research on video games and their impact has been written from a psychological research perspective. For this reason, the significance of video games and of their role in the selection and amplification of culture is almost totally ignored. The exception to this is found, as one would expect, with the researchers in communications theory and popular culture. However, their total contribution to the research literature, as indicated by the results reported in Chapter 3, is extremely limited.

In the following section, as well as in the next two chapters, I undertake an examination of the cultural content of the most popular Nintendo games currently on the market. In this analysis I am concerned not only with the general cultural messages communicated by the games, but also with their specific meaning in the context of questions related to gender stereotypes and sexual discrimination, as well as to violence and aggression.

## Nintendo's Ten Most Popular Games

Literally hundreds of games are currently available for the Nintendo Entertainment System, as well as other systems such as Sega Genesis and Activision. Examining all of the games currently available is beyond the scope of this book. After careful consideration, I determined that a representative sample of games could be isolated by taking the top ten Nintendo System games identified by *Nintendo Power* magazine in its survey of players' favorite games. This selection, which is listed in Table 4.1, is based on bimonthly polls taken by the magazine. Average scores were determined by combining the points assigned to each game in three categories: the players' survey, the survey of professionals in the video game industry (programmers, game designers, and so forth), and the survey of retailers. The polls are included as a mail-in on the back of each issue of the magazine and thus do not represent a scientific

*Table 4.1*   Top ten video games ("Player's Picks, Pros' Picks, Dealers' Picks")

| Game | Points (votes per game) |
|------|-------------------------|
| *Zelda II—The Adventure of Link* | 4,029 |
| *Super Mario Bros. 2* | 3,930 |
| *Ninja Gaiden* | 2,812 |
| *Mega Man II* | 2,266 |
| *Teenage Mutant Ninja Turtles* | 2,160 |
| *The Legend of Zelda* | 1,653 |
| *Double Dragon* | 1,401 |
| *Double Dragon II* | 1,367 |
| *RoboCop* | 1,161 |
| *Bad Dudes* | 1,113 |

*Source: Nintendo Power,* November–December 1989, p. 82.

sample of all Nintendo game players, nor of designers, programmers, and retailers. The polls do, however, provide a reasonable indication of what games are most popular among typical Nintendo game enthusiasts and in the video game industry, and they are certainly the best source of this information currently available.

In conducting the analysis of the ten most popular games drawn from the *Nintendo Power* polls, I not only played the games but reviewed the game instructions that come with the games as well as the review articles and advertisements in video game magazines such as *Nintendo Power* and *Game Players*. A brief summary of each of the ten games follows.

    *1. Zelda II—The Adventure of Link*
        Type of Game: Adventure
        Number of Players: 1
        Manufacturer: Nintendo

*Zelda II—The Adventure of Link* is the sequel to *The Adventure of Zelda*. In *Zelda II,* Princess Zelda is asleep in her palace, having been put under a spell for refusing to reveal the secret of the Triforce to the evil sorcerer Ganon. Her champion, Link, must set out on a journey across the land of Hyrule and restore six special crystals in six stone statues in a series of heavily guarded palaces. Only by doing so can Link confront the final challenge in the seventh palace, which if successfully met will allow him to awaken Zelda.

In Midoro, "the Swamp Place," Link must first pass through a cave and defeat a boomerang-wielding Goriya. Escape from the cave is only possible if he has earned the magic of the high jump. Once outside of the cave, he finds the Midoro Marsh stretching before him. Eventually he makes his way to the palace, where he is confronted by a knight in blue armor. By attacking him with a high downward thrust, he is able to defeat him. Secrets are found at various places throughout the palace that further empower Link. On the stone steps of the palace, for example, he must strike a stone statue with his sword in order to receive valuable items that will empower him in his adventures.[12]

The Land of Hyrule is a microworld in which "1-Up" dolls allow Link an extra play: fairies can restore a game player's life, jars or magic containers can add 16 points to the magic meter, a heart container can increase the heart meter by one and refill the meter to its maximum, and experience points can be stored in a treasure bag.[13] Magic, the skills of a warrior, accumulated experience, and secret knowledge are the stuff of survival and ultimately the means to victory.

 2. *Super Mario Bros. 2*
   Type of Game: Adventure
   Number of Players: 1
   Manufacturer: Nintendo

*Super Mario Bros. 2* was analyzed in detail in Chapter 2. Essentially, the second set of adventures of Mario and Luigi involve them in the task of freeing Subcon (the land of dreams) from the evil boss Wart. Monsters such as Shyguys, Hoopsters, Ninjis, Freyguys, and the three-headed Tryclyde must be overcome. Seven worlds must be traveled through before Mario is finally able to confront Wart. Items such as "Sprouts," "Stopwatches," "Cherries," "1-Ups," "Vegetables," "Mushroom Blocks," "Mushrooms,"

"Potions," "Shells," "Keys," "Bombs," "Hearts," "Pows," "Coins," and "Rockets" all play a critical role in determining whether or not Mario reaches his final goal and the confrontation with Wart.

   3. *Ninja Gaiden*
      Type of Game: Arcade
      Number of players: 1
      Manufacturer: Tecmo

*Ninja Gaiden* begins with the following Prologue: "The wind howls as the two 'Dueling' Ninjas glare at each other in the moonlight. Though these men seem like little more than shadows in the air, the moonlight reveals just for an instant, a glint of light that proves to be the end of the contest. Ken, head of the Hayabusa clan which has for generations been the guardian of the dragon sword, has been defeated."[14] Ryu, Ken's son, finds a letter after his father's defeat which tells him that if he does not return that he must go to the United States with the secret Dragon Sword. "Ryu senses danger awaiting him in America. What will be the fate of Ninja Ryu?"[15]

The October 1989 issue of *Game Player's* magazine features *Ninja Gaiden* as the "Nintendo Game of the Month." In the article, which provides a complete script of the game's action, the background of the culture of the Ninja is provided:

> In feudal Japan, one image struck fear into people unlike anything else—that of a man clad in black from head to toe. The ninjas were highly skilled fighters who wielded small arsenals of secret weapons and devices. Often they offered their deadly services to feuding warlords, who were constantly locked in a struggle for supremacy. The cloak-and-

dagger ninjas adhered to a rigid code of honor modeled after Bushido, the way of the samurai warriors. "An eye for an eye" defined their way of life.[16]

*Ninja Gaiden* incorporates not only traditional game screens but also cinema display scenes that advance the story line. In many respects, this game is similar to both *Super Mario Bros. 2* and *Zelda II* in its creation of a microworld with its own rules. As in the other two games, there is the phenomenon of the "1-Up" in which the player, by claiming a symbol on the game screen, can gain an extra life. Similarly, an hourglass, "Time Freeze," allows the player (that is, Ryu) to immobilize an enemy for up to five seconds.

Like *Super Mario Bros. 2* and *Zelda II, Ninja Gaiden* proceeds through multiple levels. Ninja lore and fighting techniques are introduced into different aspects of the game. Throwing stars, for example, are just one of the many weapons employed by Ryu. The final sequence of the game is a confrontation between Ryu and the evil Jaquio. The successful player not only defeats Jaquio but rescues Irene, the beautiful and mysterious CIA agent who appears as a key part of the story outlined in the game's cinema display scenes.

    *4. Mega Man II*
        Type of Game: Adventure
        Number of Players: 1
        Manufacturer: Capcom

*Mega Man II* is set in the future. Mega Man is a super-robot created by Dr. Light to defend against the evil Dr. Wiley. Dr. Wiley has eight super-robots of his own, each of which must be fought and defeated. Each time the player—Mega Man—destroys one of the super-robots, he gains a new power that can be used throughout the rest of the game. A final confrontation with Dr. Wiley determines whether or not the player wins the game.

    5. *Teenage Mutant Ninja Turtles*
       Type of Game: Arcade
       Number of Players: 1
       Manufacturer: Ultra Software Corporation
Teenage Mutant Ninja Turtles is based on the comic book series created by Peter Laird and Kevin Eastman. The characters are currently featured in both a television cartoon series and two motion pictures and are the basis for several lines of toys and children's clothes. They even have a breakfast cereal named after them. The characters in the comic strip are four turtles who have undergone mutation and grown large after having accidentally fallen into a pile of radioactive waste. They are named after Renaissance artists: Michelangelo, Raphael, Donatello, and Leonardo. The Teenage Mutant Ninja Turtles have a mentor named Splinter, a rat who was once human but who has been transformed into a rodent. An expert in Japanese martial arts, he is responsible for training Michelangelo, Raphael, Donatello, and Leonardo in the techniques of the Japanese Ninja.

Each of the mutant turtle characters is skilled with a different Ninja weapon. Michelangelo is an expert at using Nunchukus, Raphael the Sai, Donatello the Bo, and Leonardo the Katana Blade. All four of the turtles have a particular affection for pizza, which seems to be the main food that they live on.

The Nintendo game based on the Teenage Mutant

Ninja Turtles is a two-part adventure in which the turtles' nemesis, Shredder, has captured their human sidekick, a reporter named April. Emerging from their home in the sewers below Wall Street in New York City, they set out to rescue April and eliminate Shredder. In addition, they hope to capture Shredder's Life Transformer Gun, with which they can transform their friend Splinter from a rat back into a man.

Each turtle has different strengths and abilities. In level 1 of the game, Donatello and Raphael are the only turtles powerful enough to defeat the various enemies that are confronted. Pizza renews the strength of all the turtles and is found at various strategic points. Level 2 involves an underwater sequence in which a series of bombs must be disarmed. In level 3 the turtles are attacked by Mecha Turtle—a robot turtle. Laser soldiers attack in level 4. The huge Techno Drone and finally Shredder himself must be confronted in the final level.[17]

6. *The Legend of Zelda*
    Type of Game: Adventure
    Number of Players: 1
    Manufacturer: Nintendo

*The Legend of Zelda* is the predecessor to *Zelda II—The Adventure of Link*. The object of the game is to recover the eight missing pieces of the Triforce of Wisdom. Ganon, as is the case in *Zelda II*, is the game's nemesis and has kidnapped Princess Zelda. Players must find the Triforce pieces that have been hidden in the underground caverns of Hyrule—caverns guarded by an assortment of evil creatures. Ganon awaits the player as part of a final confrontation at Death Mountain.

### 7. *Double Dragon*
Type of Game: Arcade
Number of Players: 1 or 2
Manufacturer: Tradewest

Steven Schwartz in his *Guide to Nintendo Games* describes *Double Dragon* as being "about violence, pure and simple. The game begins with a group of thugs punching your girlfriend in the stomach and carrying her unconscious body away. Your task is to defeat everyone who stands in your way in order to secure her safe return."[18] The player assumes the role of martial arts expert Billy Lee in search of "sweet Marian," who is being held captive by the Black Warriors' mysterious Shadow Boss. In order to help him advance through the screens full of thugs, including the two Linda sisters with their whips, Lopar with his flying boxes and oil drums, Chintais with his knife, and William's bat and lit dynamite, Billy Lee has a wide range of ways to attack his enemies. Punching, head butts, elbow punches, kicks, jump kicks, low kicks, uppercuts, pin attacks, over-the-shoulder throws, spin kicks, and hair-pull kicks are just a few of the moves available to him.[19] In the final segment of the game Billy Lee (the player) confronts the Shadow Boss and attempts to rescue Marian.

### 8. *Double Dragon II*
Type of Game: Arcade
Number of Players: 1 or 2
Manufacturer: Tradewest

*Double Dragon II: The Revenge* is essentially a more complicated continuation of *Double Dragon*. Billy Lee is joined this time, however, by his former rival for sweet Marian, Jimmy Lee. Marian evidently has been killed by the Black Shadow Warriors, and the two of them are bent on revenge (it turns out that Marian is actually alive). The game begins as they head into the neighborhood controlled by the Black Shadow Warriors. Eventually they make their way to the Mansion of Terror, where the game's final scene takes place.[20]

9. *RoboCop*
  Type of Game: Arcade
  Number of Players: 1
  Manufacturer: Data East

The video game *RoboCop* is based on the 1988 movie of the same name. A sequel to the film has recently been released. A Saturday morning cartoon program based on the series is shown across the country.

The action for the film and the game takes place somewhere in the very near future. Detroit has been overcome by an epidemic of crime, and a corporate law enforcement group, O.C.P., has taken over the city to try to restore law and order. RoboCop is a half-man/half-robot, or a cyborg who was built with the brain of a fatally injured Detroit police officer. He is an enforcer, a super half-machine/half-human, whose purpose is to stop crime and punish criminals. Heavily armored with extraordinary firepower, the video game player assumes RoboCop's persona in the game, guiding him through six game levels in which he tries to bring to justice Dick Jones, the Senior Vice-President at O.C.P., who is behind almost all of the major crimes going on in Detroit. The game's instruction manual begins by explaining that

> What's going on in old Detroit isn't pretty. An epidemic of crime, violence, and death has turned it into the most lethal spot on earth—especially if you are

a cop. The government has thrown up its hands in despair and turned over the police department to the O.C.P.—a private corporation that isn't as squeamish about individual rights as elected officials are.

You're about to find yourself face to face with the malevolent Clarence Boddicker, who kills cops, slowly, as a hobby; the savage and relentless robot ED-209; and ultimately—Dick Jones, the mastermind who set all the wheels in motion.

No flesh-and-blood cop has a chance against those odds. Once upon a time, you didn't either. But that was before you became ROBOCOP.[21]

In *RoboCop* man has been transformed into machine. Law and civil order have broken down to such an extent that they can only be restored through the intervention of a private corporation that "isn't as squeamish about individual rights as elected officials are" and that uses robots rather than humans to carry out its directives.

The game consists of multiple levels. Level 1 involves the player—that is, RoboCop—"cleaning up the streets" in Detroit. Thugs fire at him from the sidewalk, windows, and rooftops. The object of the game is to get rid of as many of them as possible. Level 2 has RoboCop rescue the mayor of Detroit, who is being held captive by a disgruntled city employee. Level 3 involves the exploration of a warehouse in which "some startling discoveries" are made. In Level 4 "the drug lord, Clarence Boddicker, spills his guts to the player [RoboCop] to save his own miserable neck."[22] He explains that Dick Jones of O.C.P. is behind almost every major crime in the city; eventually the player unsuccessfully confronts Jones. Level 5 involves the player battling through the different levels of a steelworks, confronting "vicious and heavily armed scumbags" including Clarence Boddicker. Finally in Level 6 the player confronts Jones again—this time in the boardroom of the O.C.P.[23]

The film and game character avenges the death of his full human persona. He functions outside of human society, as well as outside of the law.

 10. *Bad Dudes*
   Game Type: Arcade
   Number of Players: 1 or 2 (playing in tandem)
   Manufacturer: Data East

In *Bad Dudes* the President of the United States has been kidnapped by the Dragon Ninja, "and you alone can rescue the President from his clutches. The Dragon Ninja has a helicopter waiting to spirit the President away. If he makes his getaway before you can stop him, the world will never see the President again."[24] In attempting to rescue the President, the player is faced by "wave after wave of Ninja henchmen, samurai, and super warriors."[25] Karnov, a one-time circus strongman, is a particularly dangerous foe with a talent for shooting fireballs from his mouth. A final confrontation between the player and Dragon Ninja takes place as his helicopter is about to take off with the President inside. Although weapons can be found by the player at various points throughout the game, the player primarily uses karate kicks and punches to fight his way to the final confrontation with the Ninja Dragon.

# The Importance of Play and the Meaning of Nintendo

The ten games briefly described in the previous section are of interest because of their widespread popularity, and because they can provide us with valuable examples through which to understand the social and cultural content of video games.

Paraphrasing Montaigne, we can assume that the things children play with are not simply sports, but rather should be understood as their most serious actions. Play can provide us with a significant means of understanding the world of the child—his or her needs, problems, and fears. As Bruno Bettelheim explained: "From a child's play we can gain understanding of how he sees and construes the world—what he would like it to be, what his concerns and problems are. Through his play he expresses what he would be hard pressed to put into words ... what he chooses to play at is motivated by inner processes, desires, problems, anxieties."[26] According to Bettelheim, the most important function of play and games for the child is to provide him with "a chance to work through unresolved problems of the past, to deal with pressures of the moment, and to experiment with various roles and forms of social interaction in order to determine their suitability for himself."[27] What I intend to explore here is what scenarios can be acted out and what roles can be assumed in the context of the ten Nintendo games outlined in the first part of this chapter.

The themes of rescue, revenge, and good versus evil are found in all ten of the games. In *Zelda I* and *Zelda II* the object is for Link to rescue Princess

Zelda and to recover the eight pieces of the Triforce of Wisdom *(Zelda I)* and restore the special crystals *(Zelda II)*. In *Super Mario Bros. 2* Mario and Luigi fight the Little Bosses and Wart with the goal of rescuing Princess Toadstool. In *Ninja Gaiden* Ryu avenges the death of his father and fights the evil Jaquio. In *Mega Man II* the super-robot Mega Man fights the super-robots of the evil Dr. Wiley. In *Teenage Mutant Ninja Turtles* the turtles try to rescue their pal April from the evil Shredder. In *Double Dragon* Billy tries to rescue sweet Marian from the Shadow Boss. In *Double Dragon II* sweet Marian has supposedly been murdered by her kidnappers and Billy and Jimmy Lee are set on revenge. In *RoboCop* the object is to bring the evil Dick Jones to justice and rescue the mayor. Finally, in *Bad Dudes* it is the President of the United States who must be rescued and the evil Ninja Dragon who must be defeated.

Violence is the main operative function in all of these games. In games such as *RoboCop, Double Dragon I and II,* and *Teenage Mutant Ninja Turtles*, the violence is more apparent than in ones like *Super Mario Bros. 2*. The question of whether or not the violence portrayed in these games is detrimental to the child is a difficult one to answer. Psychologists such as Bettelheim argue that children need to rid themselves of their aggressions through symbolic play.[28] He describes a situation where "some parents, out of their abhorrence of war and violence, try to control, or forbid altogether, any play with toy guns, soldiers, tanks, or other toys suggestive of war. Although these feelings toward violence are most understandable, when a parent prohibits or severely criticizes his child's gun play, whatever his conscious reasons for doing so, he is acting not for his child's benefit but solely out of adult concerns or anxieties."[29] As Bettelheim points out, just as playing with blocks does not mean that a child will become an architect, playing with guns will not determine how a child will behave in later life. In addition, playing with a toy gun can provide a child with a useful means for discharging aggressive tendencies, as well as providing an opportunity for parents to show that they trust the child and his or her actions.[30] According to Bettelheim:

> Parents who worry exclusively about shooting play often fail to take into account the duality of our human and animal natures and the distance between them. Certainly there is a great deal of the animal—and with it violence—in human beings, and sometimes these irrational forces do appear in children's games, making many parents uncomfortable. But more often it is the child's actual developing sense of humanity that motivates what seems to the uninvolved and uninformed parent to be mere brutality. Since ancient times children have played out war games in which *we* fight *them, them* being the enemy of the historical moment.[31]

It could be argued that in a game like *Bad Dudes, RoboCop,* or *Super Mario Bros. 2,* the child is able to experiment with moral identities and work through fantasies and aggressive behavior as part of a process of symbolic play. A critical element is missing, however, which is *the child's ability to define and control the conditions of play for herself.* The struggle between the forces of good and evil defined in the context of video games is narrow and circumscribed, and—what is even more important for the child—it is defined by the game developer and manufacturer instead of by the child. Thus the culture that is created for children in video games is not one that they have created for themselves; instead, it is the creation of programmers and game developers with possible links back to other media such as motion pictures and television (RoboCop the film, Teenage Mutant Ninja Turtles the comic book, television cartoon, and movie, and so on).

The extent to which a child can be shaped by the content of the games can be seen in an interview conducted with a six-year-old boy at West Laboratory School. After I announced that I was doing a book about children and Nintendo, the child being interviewed launched into the following rapid-fire description: "I know a lot about Nintendo. Well I can almost pass the whole game of Ninja Turtle Nintendo. I only have to pass three more worlds. I can almost get to the world I can't get to, because I need one more bomb to open the Hudson River. But I can't open it, but I am getting very good at it, so someday I might be able to open it. With Mario I can almost pass the whole game, but I need to get to one more fireworld." When asked why he liked the game, the child replied: "I like it because it's the funnest game. Whenever I go to Toys 'R Us I only buy Nintendo. But when they don't have Nintendo I buy Ninja Turtles instead [the figurines]." At one point this child talked about how the day before he had done "a big dance called karate." After he had demonstrated a wide range of different punches and kicks, I asked him where he had learned about karate. The little boy indicated that Nintendo was his source. When asked whether or not karate hurt people, he replied: "Of course." After an extremely detailed analysis of the game *RoboCop,* he described Teenage Mutant Ninja Turtles as his "favorite heroes on a half-shell." According to him, the Turtles were also his favorite television program.

The extent to which this six-year-old had incorporated the world of Nintendo, its reference points, characters, and metaphors, into his day-to-day life was powerfully demonstrated in a number of different ways. His reference to the turtles being his "favorite heroes on a half-shell" was a direct quote from the way they are described on television. What was really remarkable, however, was the boy's description of how he had done something wrong earlier in the day and gotten into trouble with his kindergarten teacher, whom he referred to as "the boss." On reviewing the interview, I suddenly realized that the child was describing his kindergarten class as though he were on a level of a Nintendo game such as *Super Mario Bros. 2,* and that his reference to the teacher as "boss" was to the little bosses who control the different levels of the "World of Dreams." If one extends the analogy, then the school's principal becomes the "Big Boss," Wart.

The acquisition of metaphors and images as part of the cultural configuration of many of the children who were interviewed came across clearly in a number of the interviews. A second grader, for example, while discussing in great detail the scenario of the game *Mega Man II,* explained that whether or not a "disk" was put into Mega Man (that is, a program) would determine whether he was good or evil. When the child was questioned in greater detail, it became clear that he was convinced that whether people were good or evil depended on how they were programmed, and that their programs could be changed or altered.

Many of the children clearly saw themselves as

being successful based on their mastery of various games. A six-year-old proudly described himself as "champion of the games." His repertoire included all of the Super Mario Brothers games, the Zelda games, and *Donkey Kong*. Mastery of the game was of crucial importance to this child. In describing *The Adventure of Link,* he talked in detail about the weapons used in the game, the secret information needed to win, and the triumph he felt at reaching what he described as being the ninth and final level of the game.

In the interviews just described, the children were directed by the content of the games to construct a social reality based on the games. The problem with video games such as those described in this chapter is not simply that they contain significant gender stereotypes and are often violent and aggressive, but that they allow children playing them little or no freedom to make decisions for themselves, to construct their own fantasies and in turn their own mysteries. Sherry Turkle makes this point when she argues that "when you play a video game you are a player in a game programmed by someone else. When children begin to do their own programming, they are not deciphering someone else's mystery. They become players in their own game, makers of their own mysteries, and enter into a new relationship with the computer, one in which they begin to experience it as a kind of second self."[32] Most video games—particularly those found on systems such as Nintendo—provide little or no opportunity for children to control the action themselves. Instead, they must conform strictly to the rules of the game and the program on which it is based or face defeat.

There are important qualitative differences in how

different video games are programmed, the latitude of freedom they provide the player, and the amount of control they let him exercise. This point has been made quite clearly in an article by Dan Gutman entitled "Video Games and National Character," in which he states that in video arcade games such as *Pac-Man, Space Invaders,* and *Donkey-Kong,* there are not many choices provided to the player in terms of how to proceed with the game. He concludes that these games require you to "follow the road provided for and you succeed." In contrast, games such as *Asteroids, Defender,* and *Robotron* are much more open-ended and allow the user to roam through the game, in which there are numerous paths to success or failure.[33]

This point has been made in a slightly different context by Terri Toles, who explains how, in the game *Space Invaders,*

> players who manage to memorize the idiosyncrasies of the programs can attain very high scores. The now classic "23-15 rule" of Space Invaders serves as an example: While battling rows of alien monsters, players also have an opportunity to shoot down a spaceship that flies across the top of the screen display. The number of points awarded varies, but astute players soon discovered that hitting the ship with the twenty-third shot fired and every fifteenth one thereafter earned the maximum points allotted. Such knowledge allows players to control the universe presented in a game and exhibit their mastery over it.[34]

Toles points out, however, that in order to demonstrate his mastery, the player must conform to the program that operates the game. Players are allowed only a small degree of independence or choice; conformity to the rules of the program is essential if one is to achieve the maximum number of points. According to Toles, "Few rewards for initiative and independent thought are offered."[35]

In the case of the ten games whose scenarios we have looked at in this chapter, none of them particularly rewards initiative or independent thought. The player either follows the rules exactly as defined, or she loses the game. Although characters such as Mario and Luigi in *Super Mario Bros. 2* may be presented in the game's scenario, on television, and in cartoons as being feisty and imaginative, in the actual game they are robotized characters whose actions must be carried out precisely according to the rules programmed into the computer in which the game functions.

Bettelheim has pointed to the fact that children, as well as adults, need "plenty of what in German is called *Spielraum*. Now *Spielraum* is not primarily 'a room to play in.' While the word also means that, its primary meaning is 'free scope, plenty of room'— to move not only one's elbows but also one's mind, to experiment with things and ideas at one's leisure, or, to put it colloquially, to toy with ideas."[36] Video games such as Nintendo, with their preprogrammed characters and their media-saturated images, present almost no opportunity to experiment or toy with ideas. Again, this does not need to be the case; it is a function of how the scenarios for the games function. The games do little or nothing to help the child develop an inner culture, a sense of self, an awareness that while the world provides challenges and problems, resourcefulness and the use of one's imagination and knowledge of self are an important part of being able to confront those challenges.

A critical point that has been almost completely overlooked by those involved in the development and marketing of video games is that "for a child, a game is not 'just a game' that he plays for the fun of it, or a distraction from more serious matters. For him, playing a game can be, and more often than not is, a serious undertaking; on its outcome rest his feelings of self-esteem and competence. To put it in adult terms, playing a game is a child's true reality; this takes it far beyond the boundaries of its meaning for adults."[37] By providing such limited boundaries and possibilities, the games that have been described in this chapter not only diminish but seriously limit and circumscribe how the players involved in them can define themselves and their sense of being. This is an even greater problem for girls playing the games than boys.

Of the ten games I have reviewed here, eight involve the rescue of someone. In the case of *RoboCop* it is the mayor, in *Zelda I* and *Zelda II* it is the princess Zelda, in *Ninja Gaiden* it is the CIA agent Irene, in *Teenage Mutant Ninja Turtles* it is the reporter April, in *Double Dragon* it is Marian, and in *Bad Dudes* it is the President. It is important to note that six of the eight games involving rescue scenarios have women being rescued. As I will examine in greater detail in the following chapter, the theme of women as victims is one that is repeated consistently throughout games included in the Nintendo system.

A girl playing on the Nintendo system has little or no choice but to assume the roles assigned by the programs. Of the games mentioned, only in *Super Mario Bros. 2* can the player decide whether she wants to assume the role of the princess as she sets off for the final confrontation with Wart. Is it surprising that Nintendo games have not been as popular with girls as they have with boys? Very few people like to be consistently cast in the role of the victim. Girls included in the West Laboratory interviews liked different games than the boys did, tending to prefer less violent games than those that were most popular with the boys. A sixth grade girl explained that she really liked to assume the role of the princess in *Super Mario Bros. 2,* but that she thought it was really stupid rescuing the princess in *Super Mario Bros. 1* and in *Zelda.*

Compared to the worlds of imagination provided by play with dolls and blocks, games such as those reviewed in this chapter ultimately represent impoverished cultural and sensory environments for the child. In this context, talking about educational computing, Douglas Sloan has cogently argued that we live in an era in which the "image-making capacities of the child" have been pushed aside by an educational system increasingly concerned with the development of narrowly conceived functional skills. Discussing the increasing use of computers in education, he raises a disturbing question: "What is the effect of the flat, two-dimensional, visual, and externally supplied image, and of the lifeless florid colors of the viewing screen, on the development of the young child's own *inner* capacity to bring to birth living, mobile, creative images of his own? Indeed, what effect does viewing the computer screen have on the healthy development of the growing but uninformed mind, brain and body of the child?"[38] Precisely the same arguments can be used in regard to the images found on video games such as Nintendo.

Erik Erikson has argued that play exemplifies "a specific human capacity, grounded in man's evolution and developed in the toy world of childhood imagination, namely to use objects endowed with special and symbolic meanings for the representation of an imagined scene in a circumscribed sphere."[39] As this chapter has demonstrated, the capacity of the games included in the Nintendo system to create rich and meaningful play environments is extremely limited. The Spielraum, using Bettelheim's term, provided by most video games as they currently exist is too impoverished to be of much value to our children and our culture. Video games such as Nintendo are "playgrounds," just as magic circles, card tables, arenas, the temple, or courts of justice are playgrounds in which we define ourselves and our culture. They are, as Jan Huizinga has explained, "temporary worlds within the ordinary world, dedicated to the performance of an act apart."[40]

Video games do not fulfill what Baudelaire has defined as the overriding desire of most children "to get at and *see the soul* of their toys."[41] Baudelaire asks the question: "Where is the soul of the toy?" We must ask the same question about video games: Where is the soul of Nintendo?

# 5

## The Portrayal of Women

Video games provide important insights into the values we hold as a culture. Their content reveals a great deal about our attitudes concerning violence, our fears and hopes for technology, and the social status we assign to minority groups and women. In this chapter I examine in detail how women are portrayed in the video games included in the Nintendo system.

Video games represent social and cultural "texts" that can be read and interpreted on a number of different levels. In the case of women, the way in which they are portrayed, the roles they assume in game scenarios, and the extent to which they are included as part of the action of the games provide important insights into the role and status assigned to women in our culture. In addition, by carefully examining the content of the games from a gender perspective, we can learn a great deal about how both men and women are socialized into assuming gender roles in our society. In the case of women,

Images formed from mediated percepts become part of woman's conception of herself. Mediated percepts of the status and abilities of other women (e.g., stereotypic housewives and girl Fridays in television comedies) affect her image of her own status and abilities. Plans are formed partly from images of the roles that other women play. Never seeing women in some roles and seeing women playing other roles poorly reduces the likelihood that a woman will attempt such roles herself . . . Language tells a woman she is an afterthought, a linguistic variant, an et cetera. Images shape her plans for life. Although she may be able to ignore the affronts of language, she probably cannot eliminate media images from their "construction of reality."[1]

As discussed in the previous chapter, women—when they are included at all in the games in the Nintendo system—are often cast as individuals who are acted upon rather than as initiators of action. In the most extreme manifestation of this phenomenon, women are depicted as victims in the games. This fact has important consequences not just for women but also for men, who come to assume from the images provided by the games (as well as other sources from the media and the general culture) that women are indeed the "weaker sex," and constantly in need of aid or assistance. Thus the games not only socialize women to be dependent, but also condition men to assume dominant gender roles.

Gender bias and stereotyping are evident throughout the games included in the Nintendo system. Often these appear at an obvious level that recalls the type of discrimination that was widespread in children's literature and textbooks prior to the civil rights movement of the 1960s.[2] The question arises as to why widespread gender bias of the type found in the games is tolerated. Part of the answer lies in the fact that video games are part of an invisible culture that receives little attention from the adult world. In interviews with teachers and parents conducted as part of the research for this book (see Appendix A), neither group demonstrated much knowledge of the content of the games, their scenarios, or the names and roles of characters.

The majority of the parents who were interviewed had only the vaguest idea of the content of the games and could provide only very limited descriptions of what the games were about. What came across clearly in the interviews was that although many of the parents were vaguely uneasy about Nintendo and video games in general, they accepted the fact that their children played the games. Typically, upon completing the interview, parents would ask me what my preliminary research findings showed; when I described the results reported in this and the next chapter, most parents were surprised and indicated that they had no idea that the games demonstrated particular gender bias. While they seemed more aware of the themes of violence and aggression found in the games, almost none of them seemed to be particularly aware of how widespread and pervasive these themes actually were.

The teachers interviewed, much like the parents of the children whom they taught, seemed only vaguely aware of the games and their content. A sixth grade teacher, for example, explained that she had "no direct experience with the games. I have not played the games. I would prefer that children would put more time into active pursuits—reading and other things of that sort. Outside play—we have children who almost don't play outdoors anymore, who stay inside in front of T.V. and the video games. I was just talking to a little girl right here. From three o'clock when she gets home she stays in front of that television and the video games, she doesn't play outside at all, she doesn't read for pleasure. That's her total free time occupation." Nintendo did not create significant behavior problems or difficulties for this teacher, or for other teachers included in the interviews. Although this teacher did state that she had observed one or two children make repeated references to the violence in the games, these were children whom she described as already having a proclivity toward violence.

Overall, one had the sense that video games such as Nintendo were not a subject that commanded the attention or interest of parents and teachers. In general, it seemed that they were an accepted part of contemporary childhood culture and the current revolution in computers, but not a phenomenon that parents or teachers viewed as being particularly important or worth worrying about.

A second explanation for the tolerance of gender discrimination in video games is that they function almost exclusively in the private sector. Unlike textbooks, which are subject to public scrutiny and selection, or children's books, which must pass through library approval boards, the video game market is largely controlled by the consumer—that is, the child who is purchasing a game or having it purchased for him. In this context, a walk through the aisles of a nationally based toy store chain such as Toys 'R Us is extremely revealing.

In the Toys 'R Us store that I frequented while conducting the research for this book, Nintendo-related products take up more space than any other line or type of toy in the store. One side of an entire long aisle is devoted to Nintendo games. The covers from the boxes are lined up, row upon row, with information on the games provided on the back. Order slips are conveniently located nearby. Using the order slips, customers obtain the games from the store's staff in a separate stock area. Opposite the games themselves are shelves full of Nintendo-related products, including dolls, board games, and magazines, as well as the products of competitors such as Sega. Hardware—the computers and monitors, the power gloves and portable systems such as Nintendo's Game Boy—is found in glass cases one aisle over.

While in the store to purchase games and other materials for this study, I informally observed a number of patterns of behavior. Over and over again, I saw children browsing through the games accompanied by a slightly ill at ease and confused-looking adult. Often it would be a grandparent, frequently a mother or father. The child would point to various games saying that he had heard it was "super," or that he had played it at a friend's house, or that "so-and-so has it and says it's great." The final game selection turned out to be consistently difficult for most of the children, who typically wanted to buy more than one game but who usually could afford only one because of the high cost of the games (generally $35 to $40 apiece).

Having watched this scenario many times, never once did I see an adult, or even a child, actually read the back of the game box or look carefully at its cover. Occasional questions would be asked of a store attendant, who would typically assure the adult that the game was popular and one that "the kids like to play." Many of these games blatantly portrayed sexist themes on their covers, and these same themes were typically repeated in the descriptions provided for the games. Yet never once did I hear the sexism, or the violence portrayed on the covers of the games and included in their descriptions, raised as an issue by any of the adults.

Is concern over the social content of the games exaggerated? A careful review of the games may provide an answer. In regard to the question of gender discrimination and stereotyping, the extent to which sexist themes are included in the games can be determined by an examination of their covers and introductory descriptions.

In *Double Dragon II* the cover of the game portrays Marian, Billy's kidnapped girlfriend, clutching him as he supports her with his hand wrapped around the small of her back. His other arm is entwined with a whip that he is tearing out of the hands of a woman who has enormous breasts and a punk "rooster crest" hairdo. Marian is wearing high heels. Her mini-dress is in shreds and shows the curvaceous shape of her thighs and buttocks. Her tank top is ripped at the bottom, revealing her midriff and some of her gently sloping breasts, which are pressed against Billy's muscular chest. Marian's long blonde hair cascades behind her. Her facial expression exudes an air of determination and confidence as she is held in the arms of her savior/hero Billy.

On the cover of *The Adventures of Bayou Billy*, Billy is depicted with torn jeans, an open vest, and a vicious-looking Bowie knife in his hand. The text included on the flip side of the box explains that Bayou Billy's girlfriend, Annabell, has been kidnapped by an evil city slicker named Gordon. Annabell is depicted on the cover as a smaller secondary figure. Scantily dressed, she is embraced by Gordon, who has obviously captured her.

A gender-neutral cover does not necessarily mean that a game does not contain stereotypes and discriminatory material. The back of the box for the game *River City Ransom,* for example, has the following threatening note printed on it: "To the citizens of River City: I hold your high school captive! With my gangs of students and vicious bosses roaming the streets, nobody can stop me now. Meet my demands or else!" Immediately following this text are two paragraphs that outline the context in which this ultimatum was delivered and the basic scenario for the game:

> Slick, the meanest and most powerful gang leader in River City, has issued this ultimatum—and the entire town is powerless in a grip of fear!
>
> Fortunately Alex and Ryan weren't in school the day Slick took it over. But now, their fellow students are prisoners—including Ryan's girlfriend! It's up to our two young heroes to battle their way past several dangerous city gangs, then defeat the gang lord, to free the students of River City High, and restore Peace to the panic-stricken community.[3]

Ryan's girlfriend is not even named—she is simply referred to in the possessive form as "Ryan's." The failure to specifically identify women who are being rescued occurs in other games as well. In *Dragon*

*Warrior,* for example, "the Dragon Lord has captured the princess and stolen Edric's powerful ball of light." The Dragon Lord has a distinctive title; Edric has a name; but the princess is just "the princess."

Within the closed textual schemes of the games, female victims such as Marian and Annabell, and their saviors Billy and Bayou Billy, are archetypes—emblematic figures representing basic roles that are assumed to function with both men and women. How often are these sexist themes found in the games included as part of the Nintendo system? In an attempt to answer this question, I undertook a series of content analysis studies of 47 of the most popular videogames currently available in the Nintendo system. The content of the games was analyzed at a number of different levels in terms of gender role and function. The 47 games were selected by taking the "Top 30" games rated by players, professionals (Nintendo employees), and dealers as described in Chapter 4. Although there was a great deal of agreement in their selection of the games, the three different groups selected among them a total of 47 out of a possible 90 different games. The games selected by the three groups are listed in alphabetical order in Table 5.1.

I initially analyzed the games selected in terms of the content of their covers. This was done for a number of reasons. First, I felt that the cover art of the games represented a definable unit of analysis that could be quantified relatively easily. Second, the game covers represent an attempt on the part of the game's manufacturer and developer to summarize visually the content of the game. Third, the covers of the games are widely used in conjunction with advertising for the games, both in magazines and in store displays. Essentially, the game covers represent a visual code summarizing the game and its purpose; thus they can be seen as a symbolic shorthand of the content of the game.

I then developed a scoring system for conducting a content analysis of the selected game covers based on theoretical models originally outlined by the British sociologist Erving Goffman. In his work *Gender Advertisements,* Goffman describes in detail how men and women—and more specifically women— are portrayed in popular magazine advertisements and what these advertisements tell us about issues related to gender and status in American society.[4] Goffman's study is in large part a compilation of thousands of images of women in advertising broken down into categories such as "relative size," "the feminine touch," "function ranking," "the family," "the ritualization of subordination," and "licensed withdrawal." Through the use of these categories, Goffman makes us aware of observable social phenomena within the visual frameworks of the advertising photographs.

Using Goffman's work as a starting point, I established a simple system with which to conduct a visual content analysis of the gender themes for the game covers. A single scorer was used, as was the case in Goffman's research. Although it can be argued that the use of more than one scorer would have provided inter-rater reliability scores, the themes (that is, content) were so obvious that I did not feel it was necessary to engage a second researcher. Males and females were identified by their dress and physical characteristics. Male and female figures were categorized according to whether or not they were initiating action in the visual frame—for example, striking out with a weapon, leading a group through dangerous terrain or as part of military charge. Those initiating action were identified as "dominant males" or "dominant females." "Submissive or subdued females" were identified as either being dependent or under the control of another figure in the visual frame of the cover. A final category was included in which monster, animal, mythological, or robot-type figures not identified by sex were illustrated. In those cases where a figure and its activity seemed to be identifiable in some category, but there still was some question as to identification, a question mark was placed next to the tabulations.

The results for the 47 games analyzed are shown in Table 5.1. On the 47 game covers, a total of 115 male and 9 female characters were identified. Male versus female figures predominated by a ratio of nearly 13 to 1. Twenty males were identified as having dominant poses, while no females were identified in this classification. Three females were clearly in submissive poses (one-third of the total), while no males were in corresponding representations.

The illustrations on the covers of many video games make their way, sometimes unaltered, sometimes reformatted, into advertising materials. In the March 1990 issue of *GamePro* magazine, for example, a full-page advertisement for *Double Dragon II* reproduces almost in its entirety the artwork from the cover of the game described earlier in this chapter.[5] In the same issue is another full-page advertisement for *Golgo 13,* a James Bond-type spy and adventure game, in which an attractive blonde cowers behind a man in a trench coat holding a semiautomatic pistol.[6] On the back of the magazine is an advertisement listing current video games produced by Tengen. Included with titles such as *Alien Syndrome, Road Runner,* and *After Burner* is *Rolling Thunder,* an action-adventure game set in the future in which the secret agent Leila has fallen into the hands of Mabu, an evil alien. As the Rolling Thunder organization's top-secret operative, the player has the task of rescuing both Leila and the world. The cover for the game, which is consistently used for advertisements in this and other video game magazines, shows an injured Leila in a provocative jumpsuit being carried off in the arms of the game's hero as he fires away at some unseen enemy.[7]

When a female character is subdued or kidnapped as part of the story line of a video game, more often than not the action is not illustrated on the cover of the game. In *Super Mario Bros.* Princess Toadstool is kidnapped and in need of rescue, but she is not depicted on the cover of the game. The same is true of *River City Ransom.* This observation led to a second type of analysis in which the number of times women were kidnap victims, or in need of rescue, was counted in the 47 games included as part of the Nintendo Player's Poll (Table 5.2). A total of 13 of 47 games included in the poll—or approximately 30 percent of the games—contained scenarios in which women were kidnapped or had to be rescued as a part of the game. These ratios are even more revealing when one realizes that of the 47 games included in the Nintendo Player's Poll, 11 are based on sports such as car racing, basketball, football, or professional boxing.

Rescue themes that included men were also found

*Table 5.1*    Content analysis of gender themes on the covers
              of 47 top-rated video games

| Game | M | F | DM | DF | SbM | SbF | Other |
|---|---|---|---|---|---|---|---|
| *Adventures of Bayou Billy* | 3 | 1 | | | | 1 | |
| *Bad Dudes* | 4 | | 2 | | | | |
| *Baseball Stars* | 3 | | | | | | |
| *Bases Loaded* | | | | | | | |
| *Batman* | | | | | | | |
| *Bionic Commando* | 1 | | | | | | 5 |
| *Blades of Steel* | 5 | | | | | | |
| *Blaster Master* | | | | | | | 1 |
| *Bubble Bobble* | | | | | | | 7 |
| *California Games* | 3 | 1 | | | | | |
| *Castlevania* | 2 | | | | | | |
| *Contra* | 2 | | | | | | |
| *Double Dragon* | 4 | 2 | 4 | | | | |
| *Double Dragon II* | 3 | 1 | 2 | | | 1 | |
| *Double Dribble* | 7 | | | | | | |
| *Dragon Warrior* | 1 | | | | | | 1 |
| *Faxanadu* | | | | | | | |
| *Guardian Legend* | | | | | | | 1 |
| *Hoops* | 2 | | | | | | |
| *Hudson's Adventure Island* | 1 | | | | | | 6 |
| *Jackal* | 3 | | | | | | |
| *Legacy of the Wizard* | 3 | 1 | 2 | | | | |
| *The Legend of Zelda* | | | | | | | |
| *Mega Man* | | | | | | | |
| *Mega Man II* | 4 | | 3 | | | | |
| *Metroid* | | | | | | | |

*Table 5.1* (continued)

| Game | M | F | DM | DF | SbM | SbF | Other |
|------|---|---|----|----|-----|-----|-------|
| *Mike Tyson's Punch-Out!* | 3 | | | | | | |
| *Ninja Gaiden* | 1 | | | | | | |
| *Nobunaga's Ambition* | 17 | | | | | | |
| *Operation Wolf* | 4 | | 2 | | | | |
| *Rad Racer* | | | | | | | |
| *Rampage* | | | | | | | |
| *RoboCop* | 1 | | | | | | |
| *Skate or Die* | 1 | | | | | | |
| *Strider* | 2 | | | | | | |
| *Super Dodge Ball* | 1 | | | | | | |
| *Super Mario Bros.* | 1 | | | | | | |
| *Super Mario Bros. 2* | | | | | | | |
| *Super Off Road* | | | | | | | |
| *Tecmo Bowl* | 1 | | | | | | |
| *Teenage Mutant Ninja Turtles* | 4 | | | | | | |
| *Track and Field II* | 16 | | | | | | |
| *Ultima* | 2 | 1 | 1 | | | 1 | 2 |
| *Wheel of Fortune* | | | | | | | |
| *Who Framed Roger Rabbit?* | 1 | | | | | | |
| *Wrestlemania* | 1 | | | | | | |
| *Zelda II* | | | | | | | |
| *Totals* | 115 | 9 | 28 | 0 | 0 | 3 | 23 |

*Note:* M = number of male figures on cover; F = number of female figures on cover; DM = number of dominant males on cover; DF = number of dominant females on cover; SbM = number of submissive or subdued males on cover; SbF = number of submissive or physically subdued females on cover; other = number of monster, animal, mythological, or robot-type figures with no identifiable gender

*Table 5.2*    Games that include women being kidnapped
as a major theme in 47 top-rated video games

| Game | Yes | No |
|---|---|---|
| *Adventures of Bayou Billy* | X | |
| *Bad Dudes* | X | |
| *Baseball Stars* | | X |
| *Bases Loaded* | | X |
| *Batman* | X | |
| *Bionic Commando* | | X |
| *Blades of Steel* | | X |
| *Blaster Master* | | X |
| *Bubble Bobble* | | X |
| *California Games* | | X |
| *Castlevania* | | X |
| *Contra* | | X |
| *Double Dragon* | X | |
| *Double Dragon II* | X | |
| *Double Dribble* | | X |
| *Dragon Warrior* | X | |
| *Faxanadu* | | X |
| *Guardian Legend* | | X |
| *Hoops* | | X |
| *Hudson's Adventure Island* | X | |
| *Jackal* | | X |
| *Legacy of the Wizard* | | X |
| *The Legend of Zelda* | X | |
| *Mega Man* | | X |

*Table 5.2* (continued)

| Game | Yes | No |
|------|-----|-----|
| *Mega Man II* | | X |
| *Metroid* | | X |
| *Mike Tyson's Punch-Out!* | | X |
| *Ninja Gaiden* | X | |
| *Nobunaga's Ambition* | | X |
| *Operation Wolf* | X | |
| *Rad Racer* | | X |
| *Rampage* | | X |
| *RoboCop* | | X |
| *Skate or Die* | | X |
| *Strider* | | X |
| *Super Dodge Ball* | | X |
| *Super Mario Bros.* | X | |
| *Super Mario Bros. 2* | | X |
| *Super Off Road* | | X |
| *Tecmo Bowl* | | X |
| *Teenage Mutant Ninja Turtles* | X | |
| *Track and Field II* | | X |
| *Ultima* | | X |
| *Wheel of Fortune* | | X |
| *Who Framed Roger Rabbit?* | | X |
| *Wrestlemania* | | X |
| *Zelda II* | X | |
| Totals | 13 | 34 |

in many of the 47 video games analyzed, but not nearly as frequently. Significantly, never once (according to my analysis) was a man rescued by a woman. One must question the extent to which the themes of female kidnapping, rescue, and submission pervade many children's experiences with video games.

## The Amplification of Gender Stereotypes

In the previous chapter I drew on C. A. Bowers's model of educational computing, arguing that video games are instrumentalities through which the child's understanding of her culture is mediated, and asked what it is that the computer (that is, a video game system such as Nintendo) selects for *amplification* and for *reduction*.

For at least one fifth grade girl interviewed for this book, one can see just what is amplified or reduced in her drawing of a video game. As part of a survey I conducted with children at the West Laboratory School, students were asked to draw a video game on the back of the survey they filled out. The instructions were deliberately vague; I was interested in having the students spontaneously produce their own pictorial representation of what the games were about. What is shown in the girl's drawing is her version of *Super Mario Bros. 2*, in which Princess Toadstool sits at the top of a cliff or hill, her hands folded in a "canting posture." In Goffman's schema, this gesture is characteristic of what he terms "ritual subordination." According to him, this type of configuration "can be read as an acceptance of subordination, an expression of ingratiation, submissiveness, and appeasement."[8]

Women were consistently described as being the least interesting characters in computer games by both the boys and the girls who were interviewed. When asked, for example, what he thought of the character April in the game *Teenage Mutant Ninja Turtles,* a six-year-old boy described her as being "pretty boring. She doesn't do that much. All she does is get kidnapped." In contrast, he described the Turtles as being "fun," with the word *fun* heavily emphasized by him.

To what extent does the content of games included as part of the Nintendo system reflect values more widely held in our society? Clearly no game or "text" can be completely value-free; inevitably an interpretation of the world underlies it. Video games and their content represent symbolic universes that are spontaneously consented to by the general population. In this context it can be argued that video games are instruments of a larger social, political, and cultural hegemony.

Hegemony is a difficult concept to define briefly. Raymond Williams in his essay "Base and Superstructure in Marxist Cultural Theory" argues that "hegemony supposes the existence of something which is truly total, which is not merely secondary or superstructural, like the weak sense of ideology, but which is lived at such depth, which saturates the society to such an extent, and which, as Gramsci put it, even constitutes the limit of commonsense for most people under its sway."[9] As Williams has explained, hegemony acts to "saturate" our consciousness. It is

> . . . a whole body of practices and expectations; our assignments of energy, our ordinary understanding

of man and his world. It is a set of meaning and values which as they are experienced as practices appear as reciprocally confirming. It thus constitutes a sense of reality for most people in the society, a sense of absolute because experienced (as a) reality beyond which it is very difficult for most members of a society to move in most areas of their lives. But this is not, except in the operation of a moment of abstract analysis, a static system. On the contrary, we can only understand an effective and dominant culture if we understand the real social process on which it depends: I mean the process of incorporation.[10]

Video games such as Nintendo, through a process of incorporation, have the potential to amplify certain values (for example, women as victims; women as individuals who are acted upon rather than initiating action; women as being dependent rather than independent). In doing so, the games reflect a larger cultural hegemony that functions on multiple levels.

It is not video games alone that discriminate against women; other media, including television, popular magazines, and radio, reflect similar hegemonic forces at work in the culture. What is important in the case of video games is how blatant these types of discriminatory attitudes are in terms of the content of the games.

I close with a final example of gender bias: on the cover of the recently released video game *Wall Street Kid,* the game's hero is depicted in a comic book–like representation. Dressed in a suit, holding a bag of money in one hand and a brief marked "Top Secret" in the other hand, the "Wall Street Kid" stands up to his ankles in money. Behind him is shown a blond woman in a cocktail dress, holding her hands in what Goffman would describe as a pose of ritual subordination. Ruth, the "Ruthless Lawyer," is depicted on the right-hand side of the game's cover, just above Stanley the "Crafty Consultant."

It is hard to imagine that most girls would be attracted to this game in light of its presentation of women on its cover, let alone the actual content of the game. Yet if images such as these are widespread and common, and if, as many researchers maintain, video games are an important entryway into the world of computing for children and adolescents, then women are suffering a double injustice: they are being sex-typed, and they are also being discouraged from participating in the use of computers, a fact that may put them at a significant disadvantage in terms of their future educational and job potential. In this process, not only is the existing cultural hegemony maintained—one that discriminates significantly against women—but the domain of computers becomes increasingly male-dominated.

# Aggression in Video Games

As a university teacher, I have always been impressed by the degree to which my students are linked together by their shared memories of television characters and programs, as well as by popular figures from music and film. James Bond, Bo Derek, Hoss Cartwright, "The Beaver," Led Zeppelin, and Mick Jagger are figures I can always count on as being part of my students' cultural vocabulary, while the inclusion of figures such as Rousseau, Schubert, or Aristophanes is much more problematic.[1]

Video games are playing an increasingly important role in our popular culture. As a result, they both reflect and shape our culture. The great majority of the games included in the Nintendo system are based on themes of aggression and violence. In the most common scenario found in the games, an anonymous character performs an act of aggression—typically mediated through some type of technology—against an anonymous enemy. There are no conscientious objectors in the world of video games; there is no sense of community; there are no team players. Each person is out for himself. One must shoot or be shot, consume or be consumed, fight or lose.

According to Terri Toles's work on video arcade games and American military ideology:

> The games overwhelmingly involve destruction of some sort, be it a piece of technological equipment, aliens from space or unusual monsters. Destruction of a technological artifact serves as the most common object: spaceships, aircraft, robots, missiles, ground targets, or simply "The Base" all act as suitable targets. Destruction of unidentified enemies, often from another planet, is the second most common theme; monsters, aliens or enemy soldiers attacking in hordes must be repelled.[2]

Theorists such as Martin H. Klein have explained the emphasis on violence found in many video games from a psychoanalytic point of view: "The themes of these games appear to center around the oral sado-masochistic fantasies of the fear of engulfment accompanied by its complementary reaction: aggressive tendencies. In the space games you shoot them before they shoot you; in Pac-Man you must eat them before they eat you; and in the comic character games you must assault the creature before it assaults you."[3]

Although the existence of violence and aggression in video games is an important issue, it tends to obscure the even larger context in which the violence takes place—one that involves the assumption of individual needs over those of the community. In this chapter I examine the question of violence and aggression in video games with specific reference to the question of what C. A. Bowers refers to as the "myth of individualism."

# Computers and the Myth of Individualism

Bowers argues in his book *The Cultural Dimensions of Educational Computing* that individualism is a metaphor that has been associated with profoundly different images of culture and society: "At one time the image of the individual was associated with being a subject within a feudal social order, later it was connected with being a citizen, and today it means in some quarters, being the absolute source of authority on all matters and thus a self-creating entity."[4] According to Bowers, the dominant economic and political trends in our culture tend to reinforce "a more anomic and rootless form of social relationship."[5] On an economic level this philosophy manifests itself in certain types of business entrepreneurs—more specifically, corporate acquisition or "takeover" specialists such as T. Boone Pickens, Frank Lorenzo, or Michael Milken. Through their focus on self-interest and the expansion of personal wealth—a type of individualism—it is argued that figures such as these "maintain the competitive environment necessary for social progress and for rewarding individual efforts."[6]

Bowers maintains that despite a recent revival of a sense of community in our culture, individualism remains a dominant cultural model in our society. It is reinforced by a type of education that

> . . . strengthens a form of rootless individualism by socializing students to a decontextualizing form of thinking, by ignoring the forms of knowledge and values essential to the authority of the community life and by reinforcing the liberal ideology that represents the person as an autonomous, self-directing

individual. In effect, the educational process carried on in schools may equip the individual to operate within the larger society by undermining the symbolic functions of the community.[7]

A careful examination of video games such as Nintendo suggests that the theme of individualism as identified by Bowers is the operant principle underlying the organization and structure of the majority of the games—and that the emphasis on violence and aggression found in these games is crucial to maintaining the model of the individual as an autonomous and self-directed being.

The problem of individualism in the context of computers has been dealt with by theorists other than Bowers. J. David Bolter in his book *Turing's Man* points to the profound limitations imposed by new technologies. According to Bolter, our age is unique in that both its main problems and its greatest promise come from our use of technology as a means by which to reshape nature in order to suit our needs. The key to this new technology is the computer. Turing's man, while on one level empowered by the new technology, is, on another level, ignorant of history, unaware of the natural world that surrounds him, insensitive to deeper human motives, and guided by an instrumental type of reason.[8]

The potential of video games to distort our understanding of violence and of man's inhumanity to other men, as well as the importance of context, becomes evident when one compares the content of the 1986 Academy Award–winning movie *Platoon* with the Nintendo video game of the same name. The film, which is based on the firsthand experience of its writer/director Oliver Stone, is the story of Chris

Taylor, a young recruit who has volunteered to serve in Vietnam. The story focuses on two sergeants, Barnes and Elias, who divide the allegiance of Taylor's platoon and engage in a conflict that is eventually responsible for both of their deaths.

*Platoon* is among the most powerful films ever made about the futility of war and about man's violence against and mistreatment of other men. It is a classic antiwar statement that is comparable to earlier works such as Crane's *The Red Badge of Courage* and Remarque's *All Quiet on the Western Front*. The film's message—and much of its power—is communicated in the soliloquy made by Taylor in the film's final scene:

> Looking back, we did not fight the enemy, we fought ourselves. And the enemy was in us. The war is over for me now, but it will always be there for the rest of my days. As I am sure Elias will be, fighting with Barnes for what Ron called the possession of my soul. There are times since I have felt a child born of those two fathers. But be that as it may, those of us who did make it have an obligation to build again, to teach to others what we know, and that the trial of what's left of our life is to find a goodness and meaning in this life.[9]

The Nintendo video game of *Platoon* is loosely based on the film and takes place in four different stages that include (1) the jungle and village, (2) the tunnel system, (3) the bunker, and (4) the 3-D jungle. The instructions to the game explain how the player must lead his platoon

> deep into the dense jungle and ultimately the village. Once there you will search the huts for valuable objects and trap doors to tunnels.

While in the jungle you must find the *explosives* to blow up the bridge to the village and protect your Platoon from ambush from behind. The explosives will automatically be planted on the bridge when you cross it.[10]

The game assigns five platoon members to the player, who operates in what is essentially an autonomous and independent context. When all five platoon members are destroyed the game is over. Each time a platoon member is "hit," this is recorded on an indicator at the bottom of the screen. Four hits destroy a platoon member. Morale, which is also measured on an indicator at the bottom of the screen, decreases if innocent Vietnamese villagers are shot. If six villagers are shot the game is over.

Part of the terror that is so effectively communicated in Stone's film is the suddenness with which things happen, a suddenness over which the film's main character, Taylor, and the other members of his platoon have no control. There is a constant possibility of surprise attack, of dying in an instant. In the video game *Platoon,* it is possible to suspend the game's action with a special "pause" command on the game controller. Thus in the game simulation one can stop the violence, stop the madness for a moment, and reflect on what action to take. The action climaxes with a confrontation between the player and Sergeant Barnes, who must be killed in order to win the game.

Killing innocent Vietnamese peasants is portrayed in the video game of *Platoon* as being undesirable because it will lower one's morale rating. One can take multiple hits without dying. One is able to pause while participating in the horror of war. The video game of *Platoon* severely distorts the message of Stone's film by reducing and amplifying different aspects of the film's original content. Individualism, or surviving the various conflicts, becomes the main theme of the game. This raises profoundly disturbing questions about how video games have the potential to redefine and misrepresent important cultural and social truths.

The distortion of existing cultural messages and rules—as well as the acceptance and promotion of violence—can be seen in a related context in the video hockey game *Blades of Steel*. On the surface, *Blades of Steel* is a straightforward hockey simulation. Part of the game, however, is based on fighting one's opponent. Fighting is certainly common in hockey, but it is against the rules and something for which a player is penalized. In *Blades of Steel* one is penalized—literally placed in a penalty box—for either refusing to fight or for fighting badly.

The message communicated by the rules of this video game is that violence is not only acceptable, it is necessary to win. One must strike out as an individual; one must act for oneself; one must function as an autonomous and decontextualized being. This mode of behavior would obviously be counterproductive in an actual game of hockey, but through the computer (that is, video game) it is possible to create a decontextualized microworld that conforms in its simulation to the philosophy of individualism and to a decontextualized sense of self. What *are* we teaching our children?

Much more sophisticated research needs to be undertaken that addresses the multiple levels on which video games such as Nintendo function. We need to study whether or not the games encourage violent or aggressive behavior, as well as the extent to which children playing the games assume autonomous and decontextualized definitions of self. Such research must be integrative in nature and will probably require the use of both qualitative and more traditional experimental models.

The complexity of studying how violence and aggression manifest themselves and interact with other factors is illustrated in the following quote from one of the West Laboratory School interviews with a first grade boy, who explained that he was only allowed to play Nintendo on the weekends because he got "too hypered up." He described playing a game as follows:

> When like I got up to Junior [King?] Koppa in *Mario 3*, I got up to this big guy and I had only a little knife and I was small, and I got hit because he was too fast, and I got frustrated because I didn't beat him. And then I got real hypered up, and then Mom said it was time to turn it off, and then Nicky started to have a fuss and I only cried a little bit.

Examples such as this suggest that the question of violence and aggression in video games needs to be addressed in a much more ecological/social context than has been the case in the research up to this time.

Evidence from the West Laboratory School interviews also indicates that the games, and more specifically their violent themes, are becoming integrated into the conceptual and larger world views of many children. Many of the children interviewed—virtually all of the boys—had an extensive knowledge of Ninja weaponry. This knowledge sometimes manifested itself in unexpected ways. While conducting the interviews, I informally observed a third grade composition lesson in which the teacher reviewed essays written by the children. One child presented a detailed description of weapons such as throwing stars and katangas. Significantly, despite detailed knowledge of Ninja weaponry, most of the children interviewed seemed to have little understanding of where the Ninja came from or what they signified. A fourth grade boy explained, for example, that he wasn't sure if the Ninja were Chinese or Japanese, but that the Chinese and the Japanese were the enemies because "just because they are from Japan they might want to do something different from you. And they are dangerous because they might want to fight with you." Thus the enemy is anonymous. There is no understanding of why things are the way they are—no history, no context, simply a threat and the need to act. As Terri Toles says, "The anonymity provided by the games allows the characters (and on another level, the player) to diffuse responsibility for his actions."[11]

In this context, it should not be surprising that violence is so prevalent as a theme of the games. By providing little in the way of contextual clues or variables, the world of Nintendo must depend upon force rather than reason to work through its game scenarios. It is worth noting that the ten most popular games currently available on the Nintendo system (*Zelda II, Super Mario Bros. 2, Ninja Gaiden, Mega Man II, Teenage Mutant Ninja Turtles, The Legend of Zelda, Double Dragon, Double Dragon II, RoboCop,* and *Bad Dudes*) are all based on themes of the autonomous individual acting against the forces of evil.

Although some of the games define individuals as being part of a team *(Super Mario Bros. 2* and *Teenage Mutant Ninja Turtles),* even when they do so they function separately. Thus in *Teenage Mutant Ninja Turtles* the player decides to be Raphael, Michelangelo, Donatello, or Leonardo; the turtles do not function together as a team. In this context, the actual playing of the games is an individual and autonomous act. Team playing (two or more players simultaneously on a game) is impossible in almost all of the games.

Within the theme of violence and aggression found in these games, it follows quite logically that since the player has no contextual information to guide him, he must assume the role of being either good or evil. There are no shades of gray in the world of Nintendo, no reason for people to behave badly in some situations while at other times behaving in a more positive light. Violence and aggression, whether shooting alien invaders, fighting bad dudes, or making one's way through the jungles of Vietnam, become the only viable operative principle by which the player can function. They become a substitute for personal reflection and contextual judgment.

A more detailed understanding of the predominance of violence and the theme of the autonomous self in video games included in the Nintendo system can be obtained by looking at the content of the 47 top-rated games according to the *Nintendo Power* Poll. Table 6.1 provides a brief synopsis of each game. Of the 47 video games identified by the Player's Poll, only 7 do not have violence as their major theme. Of the 40 games that do emphasize violence, virtually all are based on the principle of an autonomous individual acting on his or her own. While the

**Table 6.1**  Summary of violent versus nonviolent content in 47 top-rated video games

| Game | Description |
| --- | --- |
| *Adventures of Bayou Billy* | A 'Rajun Cajun fights his way across Southern Louisiana to rescue his girlfriend |
| *Bad Dudes* | Karate and hand-to-hand combat |
| *Baseball Stars* | Nonviolent sports game |
| *Bases Loaded* | Nonviolent sports game |
| *Batman* | Bombs, guns, the batmobile, and "electrocutioners" |
| *Bionic Commando* | Your bionic arm allows you to swing from building to building and "mow down" anyone in the way |
| *Blades of Steel* | Violent hockey simulation in which you must participate in fights or lose |
| *Blaster Master* | Drive a heavily armed armored vehicle to a final confrontation with the Plutonium Boss |
| *Bubble Bobble* | Little dinosaurs set out on their way to rescue their friend Baron von Bubba. Enemies can be destroyed by capturing them in dinosaur bubbles |
| *California Games* | Nonviolent sports game |
| *Castlevania* | To defeat the evil count and engage in a final battle with him, his body parts must be collected along with weapons such as whips |

*Table 6.1* (continued)

| Game | Description |
|------|-------------|
| *Contra* | Guerrilla warriors fight an alien invasion |
| *Double Dragon* | Karate and martial arts |
| *Double Dragon II* | Karate and martial arts |
| *Double Dribble* | Nonviolent sports game |
| *Dragon Warrior* | Karate and martial arts |
| *Faxanadu* | Adventure quest game that includes the use of magic and fighting |
| *Guardian Legend* | Alien invader game in which you must save the earth from being overrun |
| *Hoops* | Nonviolent sports game |
| *Hudson's Adventure Island* | Rescue game with weapons used to fight off wild creatures |
| *Jackal* | Machine guns and grenades in hand-to-hand combat |
| *Legacy of the Wizard* | Adventure quest game that includes the use of magic and fighting |
| *The Legend of Zelda* | Adventure quest game that includes the use of magic and fighting |
| *Mega Man* | High-tech warfare and robots |
| *Mega Man II* | High-tech warfare and robots |
| *Metroid* | Space adventure game |
| *Mike Tyson's Punch-Out!* | Boxing game |
| *Ninja Gaiden* | Karate and martial arts |

*Table 6.1* (continued)

| Game | Description |
|------|-------------|
| *Nobunaga's Ambition* | Strategic war game |
| *Operation Wolf* | Machine guns and grenades in hand-to-hand combat |
| *Rampage* | Dinosaurs and assorted monsters eat American cities |
| *RoboCop* | Robot policeman fights crime |
| *Skate or Die* | Skateboarding becomes a life-or-death sport |
| *Strider* | Secret agent game |
| *Super Dodge Ball* | Highly aggressive sports game |
| *Super Mario Bros.* | Mario fights his way to save the princess |
| *Super Mario Bros. 2* | Sequel to *Super Mario Bros.* |
| *Super Off Road* | Off road racing |
| *Tecmo Bowl* | Football simulation |
| *Teenage Mutant Ninja Turtles* | Karate and martial arts |
| *Track and Field II* | Nonviolent sports game |
| *Ultima* | Dungeons and Dragons-type game with magic and warfare |
| *Wheel of Fortune* | Nonviolent game show |
| *Who Framed Roger Rabbit?* | Rescue game following the format of a detective solving a case |
| *Wrestlemania* | Professional wrestling simulation |
| *Zelda II—The Adventure Link* | Adventure quest game that includes the use of magic and fighting |

theme of the single individual set on a quest is not a new one in Western culture, it is one that has disturbing implications. In the Arthurian legend, for example, Camelot falls because the Knights of the Round Table disregarded community and emphasized self.

It can be argued that emphasizing individualism in the games is not necessarily a problem. After all, individuals have unique characteristics that are important to value and appreciate. According to Bowers:

Viewing the self as the distinctive coming together and embodiment of the cultural and biological processes does not mean we have to adopt a reductionist view that loses sight of the *individualizing* forces that give a person's life its distinct moral, intellectual, and physical tone. Indeed, the sanctity of each person's life, each person's distinctiveness, and individual responsibility are attitudes to be highly valued. In fact, the case is being made here that an awareness of the ecology of relationships—including the unity of culture, natural environment (the air we breathe, the plants and animals we eat, the earth we walk upon, the water we drink), and biological inheritance is given individualized expression—is essential for a deeper sense of meaning, a more adequate understanding of one's place in the world and contribution to sustaining our habitat, and the enhancement of mental and physical capacities.[12]

In the end, however, the important point is that humanity and the true self are defined by their connections to culture. We cannot stand outside of the context and connections of culture and be fully realized as human beings. Video games, in their emphasis on violence and the self as an autonomous being, disregard this truth.

## Video Games and the Military

A discussion of video games and violence would not be complete without at least some reference to the military. The use of video games to recruit people into the military in our own nation is already under way. Interactive simulations are being widely used by the military to train people in the art of war. Skills such as aerial refueling, gunnery, aircraft landing, and missile launching are taught to recruits using video game formats.[13] In the early 1980s, military recruits at Fort Eustis near Williamsburg, Virginia, played a version of the arcade game *Battle Zone* that targeted realistic silhouettes of enemy tanks, helicopters, and armored personnel carriers. Consultants from Atari helped the Army create a table-top gunnery game, *MK-60,* with a price tag of $15,000 and a total of thirty separate programs.[14]

The military's attitude toward video games is extremely revealing. Major Jack Thorpe has commented, for example, that "it's important to have training devices that don't appear so obviously to be training devices."[15] In the military one is expected to take orders and obey them without question. The enemy is rarely seen, particularly in an age when most wars will not be fought hand-to-hand, but by planes dropping their bombs on anonymous populations, or by missiles being launched across the globe. Video games provide an almost perfect simulation for the actual conditions of warfare.

There is no way of knowing whether the horrors of nuclear war have become more acceptable because large numbers of people have worked through computer games such as the video arcade simulation *Missile Command*, in which missiles and destructive satellites rain down on the cities of an imaginary country. President Reagan postulated that the games probably helped prepare people for the military, a notion that seems reasonable as one looks at the scenarios of many of the games that have recently come on the market.

In *Twin Cobra*, for example, the player pilots "the world's swiftest chopper with unlimited firepower, four types of ammo, and devastating napalm bombs. Flying over military strongholds and naval barricades, you duck merciless aerial assaults, armored tank attacks, and bombard your way past heavily armed battleships. Up ahead, you see the island's menacing main defenses, loaded and ready for your arrival—if you survive."[16]

In contrast to the actual conditions of war, where surrender, compromise, or truce may be the best choice, video games promote total war and aggression. In this sense, there is literally no context for the game. The individuals being fought are part of an anonymous machine. In an advertisement in the magazine *GamePro* for the game *Conflict,* two smiling ghostlike military figures look over the shoulders of two boys at game controllers who are fighting a battle with helicopters and a tank. The advertisement reads:

At the break of dawn, the eerie sounds of heavily-laden tanks pierce the morning calm. The metallic reflection in the distance only proves that the sun is bright, but who is it?

Are these tanks the armored support you called for, or has the red machine broken through? There is little time to react. Should you wait till your men are in range, or should you attack them now?

As Commander-in-Chief, you've got no time to waste.[17]

Numerous other games, such as *Shark Attack* (a World War II simulation), *1942, Desert Commander, Nobunaga's Ambition* (a simulation of feudal warfare in sixteenth-century Japan), and *Silent Service* allow the player to act out war scenarios. Ironically, some of these games are among the very few in the Nintendo system that allow the player to deal with contextual variables: *Desert Commander* and *Nobunaga's Ambition,* for example, allow the player to consider different factors contributing to the simulation. This is particularly the case with *Nobunaga's Ambition,* which is based on the life of the Japanese *daimyo* (lord) Oda Nobunaga (1534–1582), who was responsible for the first major unification of Central Japan. In the game the player assumes the role of Nobunaga, crushing rebellions, dealing with plagues and other natural disasters, arranging political marriages, and so on.

The consistent tendency toward the depiction of violence and aggression that is so much a part of the games included in the Nintendo system works on a number of different and often subtle levels. Embedded within the violent and aggressive themes are also constructs suggesting the autonomous self as a model of action for the individual. In the context of community, as well as the larger contextual variables faced by most individuals, such a model is not only limiting but potentially dehumanizing. We must, as Bowers has pointed out, gain a greater understanding of the potential implications of a phenomenon such as Nintendo for shaping our political and moral relationships.[18] As I argue throughout this book, computers and video games are neither neutral nor without larger cultural implications.

# Conclusion

As a researcher interested in the history of toys and games, as well as a designer of both, I have always been impressed by a story written at the beginning of this century by Saki (H. H. Munro) entitled "The Toys of Peace." In the work, Saki describes an uncle who gives his young nieces and nephews a "collection of peace toys." In place of miniature lead soldiers, the children are presented with figures of famous historical personages such as John Stuart Mill, Mrs. Hemans (the poet), and Robert Raikes (the founder of the Sunday School Movement). In place of a fort the children are given a scale model of the Manchester Young Women's Christian Association. Upon receiving the gift, the children are bewildered and unsure about how they should play with it. Their uncle proceeds to suggest that they hold an imaginary parliamentary election. To this the children respond: "With rotten eggs and free fights and ever so many broken heads! . . . And noses all bleeding as drunk as can be."[1]

Despite the efforts of the uncle to discourage such bedlam, by the end of the story the children have drawn battle lines with their "peace toys." John Stuart Mill is transformed into a Napoleonic general, Robert Raikes becomes Louis XIV, and Mrs. Hemans is now Madame de Maintenon. An imaginary battle scenario is created by the children, who describe to their uncle how Louis XIV has ordered his troops to surround the Young Women's Christian Association and to capture all of the young women. Mrs. Hemans stabs John Stuart Mill (the general). The soldiers rush in to avenge his death, and a hundred of the girls are killed while an additional five hundred are dragged off to the French ships.

I have argued in the past that even though adults can present children with nonviolent and constructive toys, it is ultimately the child who will decide how he or she plays with a toy. On the surface, the analogy to Nintendo and the larger universe of video games is obvious. Yet the conditions are not the same. In the case of the children in Saki's story, they were given the means by which to reshape, as they saw fit, the "toys of peace" that they had been given. They created their own fantasy world, one which, if we follow the theories of Bettelheim, may have had therapeutic and constructive functions.[2]

In the case of Nintendo the child has almost no potential to reshape the game and its instrumental logic. There is literally one path down which the player can proceed. The machine and its program impose an instrumental logic on the play situation and the activities of the child. In light of the evidence presented in previous chapters concerning the violence, aggression, and stereotyping found in these games, this fact is particularly disturbing.

Terry Winograd and Fernando Flores raise the

question of "how a society engenders inventions whose existence in turn alters that society."[3] In order to address this question, Winograd and Flores argue that "we must step back and examine the implicit understanding of design that guides technological development within our existing tradition of thought."[4] Following their model, we can ask the question: What is a video game?[5]

Video games are a business venture for the people who manufacture and sell them. They are a means of making or losing a great deal of money at many levels. They are commercial ventures that are subject to market fluctuations. They are objects of advertising, of trade and commerce. They are the foundation on which companies like Nintendo are building a base from which to enter the field of communication and move beyond being just a toy company.

Video games are assemblies of computer chips and hardware, including video screens and controllers. They are objects which enter our households and lives, and which, as the Nintendo Corporation has planned, can act as portals to connect us to vast and powerful networks of information and entertainment.

Video games are the software and instrumental logic of the computer—the rules and procedures and limited possibilities provided by their reason.

Video games are instruments of information that serve important hegemonic functions in their perpetuation of bias and gender stereotyping.

Video games are the fusion of media; they are the potential to enter the passive medium of television and film and realize the promise of controlling and acting within the world of RoboCop, Batman, Mike Tyson, and the Teenage Mutant Ninja Turtles.

Finally, video games are a domain of inquiry in which the researcher can ask questions concerning why we are the way we are as a culture.

In reference to this final point, an important recent development is that the Media Lab at the Massachusetts Institute of Technology has accepted $3 million from Hiroshi Yamauchi and the Nintendo Corporation of Japan to fund a research center under the direction of Seymour Papert to study how video games can teach children.[6] The money from Nintendo is intended to provide the researchers at the Media Lab with the opportunity to explore two major areas. The first involves the creation of "children's work stations" capable of melding education and entertainment; the second, the further examination of "activities that teach without making kids feel as if they're being forced to learn something"— in other words, providing children, according to Papert, with the opportunity to learn much as scientists do, by experimenting.[7]

Papert and his colleagues will undoubtedly be criticized for being funded by Nintendo. Be that as it may, they have the opportunity to ask a number of crucially important questions about the world of Nintendo, including whether it should occupy the limited and at times circumscribed and prejudiced universe it is currently situated in.

I would ask Papert and his colleagues to reflect on the ideas outlined in this book. Someone needs to reinvent the world of Nintendo, to make it a world that does not cripple our capacity to act creatively and achieve a more just and equitable society. In doing so, as argued by Ernest Becker in his work *The Structure of Evil,* we need to abandon the idea of *l'homme machine* (humans as machines) and instead more actively pursue the image of *homo poeta* (humans as meaning seekers and meaning makers).[8]

We need to eliminate the violence, destruction, xenophobia, racism, and sexism that are so much a part of the world of Nintendo. We need to address in a critical way the nonneutrality of the computer and the games that function on it. Finally, we need to recognize the importance of Nintendo as a powerful symbolic and cultural form—to recognize video games as "objects endowed with special and symbolic meanings,"[9] phenomena of tremendous import and significance to our culture and its future.

# APPENDIXES
# NOTES
# BIBLIOGRAPHY
# INDEX

# *Appendix A*

# Interview and Survey Methods

In carrying out the research for this book, I employed a wide range of techniques and data collection schemes. In addition to reading theoretical sources and reviewing primary sources such as game catalogues, game magazines, and the games themselves, I felt that it would be valuable to study the roles that the games play in the day-to-day lives of children and their parents and teachers.

With this end in mind, I conducted an open-ended set of interviews with children, parents, and teachers at the West Laboratory School in Miami, Florida, during the first three weeks of May 1990. In addition, I carried out a survey of half of all the children attending the school in grades kindergarten through 5, and all the students in grade 6 (with a total of 226 students). The study was exploratory in nature and attempted to test out ideas and issues introduced in the main body of the book. Methodologically, the interviews drew on the work of G. A. Glaser and A. L. Strauss *(The Discovery of Grounded Theory: Strategies for Qualitative Research, 1967)* and used a grounded theory approach. Although I developed formal interview protocols as well as a survey instrument before undertaking the research, these were informed and modified as the research progressed. Thus, for example, the survey that was originally to be presented to kindergartners orally on a one-to-one basis was abandoned in favor of an open-ended interview approach.

The interview methods I used differed considerably according to the age of the children being interviewed. While it was possible to follow a systematic interview with the children in the fourth, fifth, and sixth grades, this became much more difficult with the younger children. In the case of the youngest group interviewed, I found that letting them talk spontaneously, with occasional probes, elicited the most information.

The West Laboratory School provided a reasonable cross section of students both ethnically and in terms of economic levels. Approximately 10 percent of the students are Hispanic, 30 percent are black non-Hispanic, and 60 percent are white non-Hispanic. Low-, middle-, and high-income groups are represented, although it should be noted that there is a great deal of competition to get into the school, which, although affiliated with the School of Education at the University of Miami, is a Dade County Public School.

Survey data across the grades proved cumulatively unreliable. The younger children, as might be expected, had a very difficult time explaining how much television they watched per week, or how often they played Nintendo or other video games. In the case of the older children, the survey data seemed more reliable: the figures reported by the older students in their surveys were reconfirmed in their interviews. Since the younger children's information on how many hours they actually watched television and played video games per week did not prove to be reliable, I did not include these data in the study.

With the exception of the table included in Appendix B, the results of the survey and interviews are reported in the main text of this book. Although my original intention was to include both the survey and interview data in a penultimate chapter, I concluded that the information from the survey and interviews—in particular the latter—would be more useful if it were introduced as examples in those sections of the book where a particular issue was being emphasized or discussed. The data from the West Laboratory study are obviously of a preliminary nature and should be interpreted as such. The West Laboratory material should not be construed in any way as representing the main focus of this book, but instead should be understood as a suggestive preliminary or pilot study.

Half of the classes in the school were randomly chosen for the study. The combination of the kindergarten group into a single large class under two teachers necessitated the use of a class list in which every other student on the list was drawn for the interview. The survey was not conducted with the kindergarten students. Both sixth grade classes were surveyed—more a matter of accident and convenience than design; I felt that including the results from both classes did not pose a problem in reporting the results for this study.

After scanning the survey results, I contacted those children who reported playing a minimum of five hours of video games a week about participating in the study. Notes requesting permission to have the children interviewed were sent home; approximately half of the parents responded to the request, most also giving permission to be interviewed themselves (a total of 22 permissions were received). I interviewed a total of 21 children and also conducted a limited number of parent and teacher interviews.

The use of such techniques, while systematic and carefully reasoned, should not be interpreted as scientific but rather as exploratory in nature, involving qualitative judgments on the part of the researcher— judgments suggested by the natural setting in which the research was conducted. Future research demands intensive observational studies of children who play video games, focusing on questions of their impact on family interaction, study habits, personal development, and relationships, as well as longitudinal studies on the role of the games in shaping attitudes and belief systems.

## *Appendix B*

# Survey of Video Game Ownership

This survey, taken in classrooms in grades 1–6 at the West Laboratory School, clearly demonstrates the degree to which Nintendo is an important part of the lives of many children. When asked "Do you own a video game system like Nintendo?" only 9 out of 86 boys who responded to the survey said no, while 31 out of 92 girls said no. Breakdowns of these figures on a grade by grade level are shown in the following table.

Students' responses to the question: Do you own a video game system like Nintendo?

| Grade | Yes | No |
|---|---|---|
| First grade | | |
| Males | 14 | 0 |
| Females | 7 | 5 |
| Second grade | | |
| Males | 13 | 3 |
| Females | 7 | 3 |
| Third grade | | |
| Males | 10 | 4 |
| Females | 10 | 4 |
| Fourth grade | | |
| Males | 9 | 0 |
| Females | 9 | 4 |
| Fifth grade | | |
| Males | 16 | 0 |
| Females | 7 | 3 |

| Grade | Yes | No |
|---|---|---|
| Sixth grade (both classes) | | |
|    Males | 24 | 2 |
|    Females | 21 | 12 |
| | | |
| Totals | | |
|    Males | 86 | 9 |
|    Females | 61 | 31 |

# Notes

## Introduction

1. Virtual reality links the computer user much more directly to the action of a computer game or program than has been possible in the past. Using a power glove goes beyond the manipulation of a joystick in that the user actually feels that he is part of the action of the program with which he is interacting. For further discussions of this and related technologies, see Stewart Brand, *The Media Lab: Inventing the Future at MIT.* (New York: Penguin Books, 1988), and Steven Levy, "Brave New World," *Rolling Stone,* June 14, 1990, pp. 92–100.
2. Nintendo of America, Inc., *Nintendo "Pocket Power"* (New York: EMCI, Limited, 1989), p. 20.
3. Ibid., pp. 38–39.
4. Ibid., p. 38.
5. Ibid., p. 39.

## 1. The Video Game Market

1. Donna Leccese, "Video Games Go Back to the Future," *Playthings,* June 1988, p. 84.
2. "Nintendo Scored Record Sales in 1990," *The Miami Herald,* January 11, 1991.
3. Leccese, "Video Games Go Back to the Future."
4. Marshall B. Jones, "Video Games as Psychological Tests," *Simulation and Games,* vol. 15, no. 2 (June 1984), 133.
5. Ibid., p. 134.

6. Claude Braun, Georgette Goupil, Josette Giroux, and Yves Chagon, "Adolescents and Microcomputers: Sex Differences, Proxemics, Task and Stimulus Variables," *Journal of Psychology,* vol. 120, no. 6 (1986), 530.

7. Leccese, "Video Games Go Back to the Future," p. 33.

8. Katherine Carlon, "Video Game Market Sharpens Focus," *Playthings,* June 1988, p. 30.

9. Leccese, "Video Games Go Back to the Future," p. 32; *The Miami Herald,* "Nintendo Scored Record Sales in 1990"; Teresa Salas, "Video Game Market Continues to Shine," *Playthings,* January 1990, p. 39.

10. Leccese, "Video Games Go Back to the Future," p. 32.

11. Ibid., p. 88.

12. Ibid., p. 32.

13. Ibid.

14. "*Playthings* Retail Survey of Best-Selling Toys," *Playthings,* May 5, 1989, p. 22.

15. Ibid.

16. Donna Leccese, "Retailers Say Video Is a Dream Come True," *Playthings,* May 5, 1989, p. 32.

17. Ibid.

18. Ibid.

19. Ron Givens, "Boys and Dolls in Toyland," *Newsweek,* November 27, 1989, p. 99.

20. Peter Main, "*Playthings* Panel Peers into the 1990s," *Playthings,* May 5, 1989, p. 42.

21. Ibid.

22. Tom Panelas, "Adolescents and Video Games: Consumption of Leisure and the Social Construction of the Peer Group," *Youth and Society,* vol. 15, no. 1 (September 1983), 52.

23. Ibid.

24. "Top Secret Tips," The Topps Company, Inc., 1989, included as part of the *Nintendo Cereal System.*

25. Panelas, "Adolescents and Video Games," p. 59.

26. Ibid., p. 60.

27. Jeff Rovin, *How to Win at Nintendo Games #2* (New York: St. Martin's Press, 1989).

28. Ibid., back cover page.

29. Promotional advertisement entitled "*Game Player's:* The Magazine for Every Video or Computer Game Player," *Game Player's Buyer's Guide to Nintendo Games,* vol. 2, no. 5 (1989), 28–29.

30. "Take This Perfect Gift Home!" Brochure produced by Nintendo Corporation of America advertising their magazine *Nintendo Power,* n.d.

31. "Better Blasters Master Faster with Official *Game Player's Gametapes,*" *Game Player's Buyer's Guide to Nintendo Games,* vol. 2, no. 5 (1989), 44–45.

32. "There's No Match for WWF Wrestlemania," full-page advertisement, *Game Player's,* June/July 1989, p. 9.

33. "RoboCop," advertisement included on the back cover of *Game Player's* magazine, October 1989.

34. Jason R. Rich, "Face to Face with Danny Pintauro," *Game Player's,* October 1989, p. 25.

35. "Celebrity Profiles: Karch Kiraly," *Nintendo Power,* January/February 1989, p. 95.

36. Sherry Turkle, *The Second Self: Computers and the Human Spirit* (New York: Simon and Schuster, 1984), p. 83.

37. Ibid.

38. Ibid., p. 82.

39. Ibid.

40. Terri Toles, "Video Games and American Military Ideology," in *Critical Communications Review, Vol. III: Popular Culture and Media Events,* ed. Vincent Mosco and Janet Wasko (Norwood, N.J.: Ablex, 1985), p. 211.

41. "Nintendo Accused of Cornering Market," *The Miami Herald,* Friday, December 9, 1989.

42. Ibid.

43. Leccese, "Video Games Go Back to the Future," p. 86.

44. "Nintendo vs. Video Renters," *Television Digest,* August 14, 1989, p. 13.

45. "Nintendo Legal Battles," *Television Digest,* March 13, 1989, p. 17.
46. "Nintendo Expects Network with AT&T by 1991," *Television Digest,* August 21, 1989, p. 11.
47. "Nintendo Financial Network," *Television Digest,* October 9, 1989, p. 15.
48. Ibid.
49. Givens, "Boys and Dolls in Toyland," p. 99.

## 2. Video Games as Microworlds

1. Marshall McLuhan, *Understanding Media: The Extensions of Man* (New York: McGraw-Hill, 1964), p. 7.
2. Ibid., p. 235.
3. Ibid., p. 237.
4. Bruno Bettelheim, *The Uses of Enchantment: The Meaning and Importance of Fairy Tales* (New York: Alfred Knopf, 1976), p. 3.
5. Ibid.
6. Ibid., p. 5.
7. Ibid., p. 6.
8. McLuhan, *Understanding Media,* p. 238.
9. Frederick Williams, *The Communications Revolution* (Beverly Hills, Calif.: Sage Publications, 1982), p. 18.
10. Godfrey J. Ellis, "Youth in the Electronic Environment: An Introduction," *Youth and Society,* vol. 15, no. 1 (September 1983), 4.
11. Ibid., p. 5.
12. Ibid., pp. 8–9.
13. Ibid., p. 10.
14. C. A. Bowers, *The Cultural Dimensions of Educational Computing* (New York: Teachers College Press, 1980), p. 2.
15. Ibid., p. 3.
16. Marshall B. Jones, "Video Games as Psychological Tests," *Simulation and Games,* vol. 15, no. 2 (June 1984), 132.

17. Ibid.
18. Ibid.
19. Ibid.
20. Sherry Turkle, *The Second Self: Computers and the Human Spirit* (New York: Simon and Schuster, 1984), p. 68.
21. According to Robert McClintock: "Digital technologies do not transmit one thing that is analogous to another, the real matter in question. Rather, a digital technology transmits exact, or nearly exact, values, as precisely as these can be represented in binary code . . . The key to digital technology, compared with analog, is the digital lack of ambiguity: It deals with successive states, either-or conditions in which a circuit is either off or on. In contrast, the analog technology deals endlessly with the torturing indefinite in which each successive state differs from its predecessor by a nearly infinitesimal increment. The analog approximates one whole with another; the digital samples the whole and recreates it from that sampling." Robert McClintock, "Marking the Second Frontier," *Teachers College Record*, vol. 89, no. 3 (Spring 1988), 346.
22. In the interviews conducted with parents and teachers for this book, comparisons between pinball arcade games and video games were made by several different people. Remembering back to his childhood, one parent likened video games to "just another form of pinball." This comparison, however, fails to take into account the significantly different technologies underlying each type of game. It may be that many parents and teachers are less critical than they might be of digital systems such as Nintendo because they simply see them as extensions of the earlier analog system of pinball.
23. Jones, "Video Games as Psychological Tests," p. 133.
24. Turkle, *The Second Self,* p. 69. Marshall Jones in his article "Video Games as Psychological Tests," p. 133, makes the same point to the effect that "video games do not model familiar physical systems. To a large extent

the rules of the game are arbitrary; they create their own world, with its own laws of motion, and frequently this new world is fresh and engaging."

25. Turkle, *The Second Self,* p. 71.
26. Ibid., p. 65.
27. Ibid., pp. 87–88.
28. Ibid., p. 66.
29. Ibid.
30. Ibid., p. 82.
31. See Thomas W. Malone, "What Makes Things Fun to Learn? A Study of Intrinsically Motivating Computer Games," Xerox Palo Alto Research Centre, Cognitive and Instructional Sciences Series (August 1980); Malone, "What Makes Computer Games Fun?" BYTE, December 1981, pp. 258–277; and Malone, "Toward a Theory of Intrinsically Motivating Instruction," *Cognitive Science,* vol. 5, no. 4 (1981). The research described in these studies was the basis for Malone's doctoral dissertation in psychology at Stanford University.
32. Malone, "What Makes Computer Games Fun?" p. 258.
33. Ibid. See also Malone, "Toward a Theory of Intrinsically Motivating Instruction," pp. 333–369.
34. Malone, "What Makes Computer Games Fun?" p. 258.
35. "Super Mario Bros. 2," *Nintendo Power,* July/August 1988, p. 6.
36. Ibid., p. 7.
37. Ibid.
38. Ibid.
39. Ibid.
40. Ibid., p. 10.
41. Ibid.
42. Ibid.
43. Ibid., p. 6.
44. Ibid., p. 11.
45. Ibid., p. 10.
46. Seymour Papert, *Mindstorms: Children, Computers, and Powerful Ideas* (New York: Basic Books, 1980), p. 12.

47. Patricia Marks Greenfield, *Mind and Media: The Effects of Television, Video Games, and Computers* (Cambridge, Mass.: Harvard University Press, 1984), p. 101.

### 3. Research on Video Games

1. G. W. Selnow, "Playing Videogames: The Electronic Friend," *Journal of Communication,* vol. 34 (1984), 148.
2. Quoted in J. R. Dominick, "Videogames, Television Violence, and Aggression in Teenagers," *Journal of Communication,* vol. 34 (1984), 136.
3. "Games That People Play," *Time,* January 18, 1982, p. 52.
4. Ibid., p. 53.
5. "Top 30," *Nintendo Power,* November/December 1989, p. 81.
6. "Bionic Commando," *Game Player's Buyers Guide to Nintendo Games,* vol. 2, no. 5 (n.d.), 42.
7. "Rampage," *Game Player's Buyer's Guide to Nintendo Games,* vol. 2, no. 5 (n.d.), 66. A seven-year-old included in the interview study at West Laboratory School, when asked to design an ideal video game, explained that he would want a "game like Rampage, only you got to destroy cities all over the world, not just in America."
8. "Escape from the Prison Camp of Ordinary Games," advertisement included in *Game Player's Strategy Guide: Nintendo Games* (Greensboro, N.C.: Signal Publications, 1989), p. 21.
9. Terry Toles, "Video Games and American Military Ideology," in *The Critical Communications Review, Vol. III: Popular Culture and Media Events,* ed. Vincent Mosco and Janet Wasko (Norwood, N.J.: Ablex, 1985), p. 211.
10. G. D. Gibb, J. R. Bailey, T. T. Lornbirth, and W. P. Wilson, "Personality Differences between High and Low Electronic Video Game Users," *Journal of Psychology,* vol. 114 (1983), 143–152.
11. B. D. Brooks [untitled], in S. S. Baughman and P. D. Cla-

gett, eds., "Video Games and Human Development: A Research Agenda for the '80s," Papers and Proceedings of the Symposium Held at Harvard Graduate School of Education, Cambridge, Massachusetts (Gutman Library, Harvard Graduate School of Education, 1983). Cited in E. A. Egli and L. S. Meyers, "The Role of Video Game Playing in Adolescent Life: Is There Reason to be Concerned?" *Bulletin of the Psychonomic Society,* vol. 22, no. 4 (1984), 309.

12. Egli and Meyers, "The Role of Video Game Playing in Adolescent Life," pp. 309–312.

13. Edna Mitchell, "The Dynamics of Family Interaction around Home Video Games," *Marriage and Family Review,* vol. 8, nos. 1 and 2 (Spring 1985), 121–135.

14. Ibid., p. 132.

15. Martin H. Klein, "The Bite of Pac-Man," *Journal of Psychohistory,* vol. 2, no. 3 (Winter 1984), 395.

16. Ibid., p. 398.

17. Ibid., p. 399.

18. Ibid.

19. Ibid., p. 400.

20. Gerald I. Kestenbaum and Lissa Weinstein, "Personality, Psychopathology, and Developmental Issues in Male Adolescent Game Use," *Journal of the American Academy of Child Psychiatry,* vol. 24, no. 3 (1985), 330.

21. Ibid.

22. Bruno M. Kappes and Dan L. Thompson, "Biofeedback vs. Video Games: Effects of Impulsivity, Locus of Control, and Self-Concept with Incarcerated Juveniles," *Journal of Clinical Psychology,* vol. 41, no. 5 (September 1985), 698–706.

23. Tom Panelas, "Adolescents and Video Games: Consumption of Leisure and the Social Construction of the Peer Group," *Youth and Society,* vol. 15, no. 1 (September 1983), 62.

24. Ibid., pp. 62–63.

25. Desmond Ellis, "Video Arcades, Youth, and Trouble," *Youth and Society,* vol. 16, no. 1 (September 1984), 51.
26. Kestenbaum and Weinstein, "Personality, Psychopathology, and Developmental Issues," p. 329.
27. Henry Morlock, Todd Yando, and Karen Nigolean, "Motivation of Video Game Players," *Psychological Reports,* vol. 57 (1985), 250.
28. S. Kiesler, L. Sproull, and J. S. Eccles, "Second Class Citizens," *Psychology Today,* vol. 17, no. 3 (1983), 42.
29. Ibid., p. 42.
30. Toles, "Video Games and American Military Ideology," p. 214.
31. Kiesler, Sproull, and Eccles, "Second Class Citizens," p. 42.
32. Ibid., p. 46.
33. Ibid., p. 47.
34. Dan Gutman, "Finding an Heir for Pac-Man," *Psychology Today,* vol. 17 (March 1983), 10.
35. Gary W. Selnow and Hal Reynolds, "Some Opportunity Costs of Television Viewing," *Journal of Broadcasting,* in press.
36. John Robinson, "Television and Leisure Time: A New Scenario," *Journal of Communication,* vol. 31, no. 1 (Winter 1981), 120–130.
37. Selnow, "Playing Videogames," pp. 148–156.
38. Bradley Greenberg, "Gratification of Television Viewing and Their Correlates for British Children," in Jay Blumler and Elihu Katz, eds., *The Uses of Mass Communications* (Beverly Hills, Calif.: Sage, 1974), pp. 71–92.
39. Selnow, "Playing Videogames," p. 153.
40. Ibid., p. 155.
41. Ibid., p. 155–156.
42. Marshall McLuhan, *Understanding Media: The Extensions of Man* (New York: McGraw-Hill, 1964), p. 243.
43. Dominick, "Videogames, Television Violence, and Aggression in Teenagers," p. 138.

44. Ibid.
45. "Thundercade," advertisement included in *Game Player's Strategy Guide: Nintendo Games* (Greensboro, N.C.: Signal Publications, 1989), p. 37.
46. Bill Marcus, "Preview *(Shinobi)*," *Game Pro Magazine*, 1989, p. 24.
47. "The Wait Is Over, Power Glove and U-Force Debut!" *Game Player's Strategy Guide* (Greensboro, N.C.: Signal Research, 1989), p. 124.
48. Dominick, "Videogames, Television Violence, and Aggression in Teenagers," p. 138.
49. Joel Cooper and Diane Mackie, "Video Games and Aggression in Children," *Journal of Applied Social Psychology,* vol. 16, no. 8 (1986), 726–744.
50. Craig A. Anderson and Catherine M. Ford, "Affect of the Game Player: Short-Term Effects of Highly and Mildly Aggressive Video Games," *Personality and Social Psychology Bulletin,* vol. 12, no. 4 (December 1986), 390–402.
51. Steven B. Silvern and Peter A. Williamson, "The Effects of Video Game Play on Young Children's Aggression, Fantasy, and Prosocial Behavior," *Journal of Applied Developmental Psychology,* vol. 8 (October-December 1987), 453–462.
52. P. J. Favaro, "The Effects of Video Game Play on Mood, Physiological Arousal, and Psychomotor Performance," Ph.D. dissertation, Hofstra University, 1983.
53. Daniel Graybill, Janis R. Kirsch, and Edward E. Esselman, "Effects of Playing Violent versus Nonviolent Video Games on the Aggressive Ideation of Aggressive and Nonaggressive Children," *Child Study Journal,* vol. 15, no. 3 (1985), 199–205.
54. Daniel Graybill, Marilyn Strawniak, Teri Hunter, and Margaret O'Leary, "Effects of Playing versus Observing Violent versus Nonviolent Video Games on Children's Aggression," *Psychology: A Quarterly Journal of Human Behavior,* vol. 24, no. 3 (1987), 1–8.

## 4. Play and the Cultural Content of Games

1. Terri Toles, "Video Games and American Military Ideology," in *The Critical Communications Review, Vol. III: Popular Culture and Media Events,* ed. Vincent Mosco and Janet Wasko (Norwood, N.J.: Ablex, 1985), p. 211.
2. Marshall McLuhan, *Understanding Media: The Extensions of Man* (New York: McGraw-Hill, 1964), p. 245.
3. Ibid, p. 238.
4. Ibid.
5. Ibid., p. 242.
6. Toles, "Video Games and American Military Ideology," pp. 211–212. A related comment by Roland Barthes concerning toys makes a similar argument: "All the toys one commonly sees are essentially a microcosm of the adult world; they are reduced copies of human objects, as if in the eyes of the public the child was, all told, nothing but a smaller man, a homunculus to whom must be supplied objects of his own size." See the essay "Toys," included in *Mythologies,* selected and translated from the French by Annette Lavers (Boston: Hill and Wang, 1972), p. 53.
7. Tom Panelas, "Adolescents and Video Games: Consumption of Leisure and the Social Construction of the Peer Group," *Youth and Society,* vol. 15, no. 1 (September 1983), 64.
8. C. A. Bowers, *The Cultural Dimensions of Educational Computing: Understanding the Non-Neutrality of Technology* (New York: Teachers College Press, 1980), p. 24.
9. Ibid.
10. Ibid., p. 27.
11. Ibid., pp. 32–33.
12. "The Adventure of Link, Zelda II," *Nintendo Power,* January/February 1989, pp. 18–34.
13. Ibid., p. 8.
14. *Nin-Ja Gaiden Instructions* (Tecmo, Inc., 1989), p. 3.
15. Ibid.

16. "Nintendo Game of the Month: Ninja Gaiden," *Game Players,* October 1989, p. 55.

17. "At Last! Teenage Mutant Ninja Turtles Is Released! History and Hints of Those Hard-Shelled Crime Fighters," *Game Player's Buyer's Guide: Nintendo Games,* vol. 2, no. 5 (1989), 8, 12, 14, 18, 23–24, 26.

18. Steven Schwartz, *Compute's Guide to Nintendo Games* (Radnor, Pa.: Compute! Books, 1989), p. 56.

19. "Double Dragon: Street Toughs Move to Attack," *Nintendo Power,* July–August 1988, p. 63.

20. "Double Dragon II: The Revenge," *Nintendo Power,* January/February 1990, pp. 30–35.

21. *RoboCop: Instruction Manual* (San Jose, Calif.: Data East, 1988).

22. Ibid.

23. Ibid.

24. *Bad Dudes Instruction Manual* (San Jose, Calif.: Data East, 1988), p. 2.

25. Ibid.

26. Bruno Bettelheim, "The Importance of Play," *Atlantic Monthly,* March 1987, p. 35.

27. Ibid., p. 38.

28. Ibid., p. 43.

29. Ibid., p. 45.

30. Ibid.

31. Ibid., p. 46.

32. Sherry Turkle, *The Second Self: Computers and the Human Spirit* (New York: Simon and Schuster, 1984), p. 92.

33. Dan Gutman, "Video Games and National Character," *Psychology Today,* March 1983, p. 9.

34. Toles, "Video Games and American Military Ideology," p. 208.

35. Ibid.

36. Bettelheim, "The Importance of Play," p. 37.

37. Ibid., p. 35.

38. Douglas Sloan, "For the Record," *Teachers College Record,* vol. 85, no. 4 (Summer 1984), 539–547.

39. Ibid.
40. Quoted in Erik H. Erikson, *Toys and Reasons: Stages in the Ritualization of Experience* (New York: W. W. Norton, 1977), p. 43.
41. Charles Baudelaire, "A Philosophy of Toys," in *The Painter of Modern Life and Other Essays,* trans. and ed. Jonathan Mayne (New York: Da Capo Press, 1986), p. 203.

## 5. The Portrayal of Women

1. M. Butler and W. Paisley, *Woman and the Mass Media: Sourcebook for Research and Action* (New York: Human Sciences Press, 1980), pp. 49–50.
2. For an analysis of the discriminatory content of the literature from this period, see Catherine Ross, "Sex-Role Socialization in Picture Books for Preschool Children," *American Journal of Sociology,* vol. 77, no. 6 (1972), 1125–1150.
3. Back cover of the computer game *River City Ransom* (American Technos Inc.).
4. Erving Goffman, *Gender Advertisements* (New York: Harper and Row, 1976).
5. "Aklaim Presents *Double Dragon II, The Revenge*—A Martial Arts Explosion," *GamePro,* vol. 2, no. 3 (March 1990), 11.
6. "An Encore Performance," *GamePro,* vol. 2, no. 3 (March 1990), 21.
7. "Fly Away with the Best," *GamePro,* vol. 2, no. 3 (March 1990), back cover.
8. Goffman, *Gender Advertisements,* p. 46.
9. Raymond Williams, "Base and Superstructure in Marxist Cultural Theory" in *Schooling and Capitalism: A Sociological Reader* (London: Routledge and Kegan Paul, 1976), pp. 204–205.
10. Ibid., p. 205. My understanding of hegemony and its implications for education also draws heavily on the work

of Michael Apple. See his studies *Ideology and Curriculum* (London: Routledge and Kegan Paul, 1979); *Cultural and Economic Reproduction in Education: Essays on Class, Ideology and the State* (London: Routledge and Kegan Paul, 1982); *Education and Power* (Boston: Routledge and Kegan Paul, 1983); and *Ideology and Practice in Schooling,* ed. Michael W. Apple and Lois Weis (Philadelphia: Temple University Press, 1983).

## 6. Aggression in Video Games

1. In his essay "Boys' Weeklies" George Orwell commented that "to what extent people draw their ideas from fiction is disputable. Personally I believe that most people are influenced far more than they would care to admit by novels, serial stories, films and so forth, and that from this point of view the worst books are often the most important, because they are usually the ones that are read earliest in life. It is probable that many people who would consider themselves extremely sophisticated and 'advanced' are actually carrying through life an imaginative background which they acquired in childhood." See George Orwell, "Boys' Weeklies," in *An Age Like This, 1920–1940 (The Collected Essays, Journalism, and Letters of George Orwell,* vol. 1*),* ed. Sonia Orwell and Ian Angus (New York: Harcourt, Brace and World, 1968), p. 482.

2. Terri Toles, "Video Games and American Military Ideology," in *The Critical Communications Review, Vol. III: Popular Culture and Media Events,* ed. Vincent Mosco and Janet Wasko (Norwood, N.J.: Ablex, 1985), p. 215.

3. Martin H. Klein, "The Bite of Pac-Man," *Journal of Psychology,* vol. 11 (Winter 1984), 399.

4. C. A. Bowers, *The Cultural Dimensions of Educational Computing: Understanding the Non-Neutrality of Technology* (New York: Teachers College Press, 1980), p. 12.

5. Ibid., p. 13.

6. Ibid., p. 12.
7. Ibid., p. 13.
8. See J. David Bolter, *Turing's Man: Western Culture in the Computer Age* (Chapel Hill: University of North Carolina Press, 1984).
9. Oliver Stone, *Platoon* (Hemdale Film Corporation, 1986).
10. *Platoon: Instruction Manual* (Wood Dale, Ill.: Sunsoft, 1988), p. 3.
11. Toles, "Video Games and American Military Ideology," p. 217.
12. Bowers, *The Cultural Dimensions of Educational Computing,* pp. 77–78.
13. G. W. Selnow, "Playing Videogames: The Electronic Friend," *Journal of Communication,* vol. 34 (1984), 148.
14. Cited in J. R. Dominick, "Videogames, Television Violence, and Aggression in Teenagers," *Journal of Communication,* vol. 34 (1984), 136.
15. Ibid.
16. "Twin Cobra," *GamePro,* vol. 2, no. 3 (March 1990), 55.
17. "Prepare Yourself for Conflict," *GamePro,* vol. 2, no. 3 (March 1990), 19.
18. Bowers, *The Cultural Dimensions of Educational Computing,* p. 78.

## Conclusion

1. H. H. Munro (Saki), "The Toys of Peace," in *The Short Stories of Saki* (New York: Modern Library, 1951), p. 444.
2. As Bettelheim argues: "The fairy tale is therapeutic because the patient finds his *own* solutions, through contemplating what the story seems to imply about him and his inner conflicts at this moment in his life." See Bruno Bettelheim, *The Uses of Enchantment* (New York: Alfred A. Knopf, 1976), p. 25.
3. Terry Winograd and Fernando Flores, *Understanding*

*Computers and Cognition: A New Foundation for Design* (Reading, Mass.: Addison-Wesley, 1987), p. 4.

4. Ibid., p. 5.
5. Winograd and Flores ask the question: "What is a word processor?" According to them, "The first thing to recognize is that different answers grow from the concerns of different individuals. For the manager of a factory that builds word processors, they are assemblies of electronic and mechanical devices, to be constructed, tested, and shipped. For the person who programs the word processor, it is a particular collection of software, dealing with the input, storage, and output of bytes of information. It operates through some kind of interface to a user who generates and modifies that information" (ibid.).
6. Lawrence Edelman, "MIT, Nintendo to Mix Playing with Teaching," *Boston Globe,* May 16, 1990.
7. Ibid.
8. Ernest Becker, *The Structure of Evil: An Essay on the Unification of the Science of Man* (New York: George Braziller, 1968), pp. 169–176.
9. Erik H. Erikson, *Toys and Reasons: Stages in the Ritualization of Experience* (New York: W. W. Norton, 1977), p. 43.

# Bibliography

"The Adventure of Link, Zelda II." *Nintendo Power* (January/
February 1989): 18–34.

"Aklaim Presents *Double Dragon II, The Revenge*—A Martial
Arts Explosion." *GamePro*, 2;3 (March 1990): 11.

Allen, Woody. "The Kugelmas Episode." *The New Yorker,* May
2, 1977.

"An Encore Performance." *GamePro,* 2;3 (March 1990): 21.

Anderson, Craig A., and Catherine M. Ford. "Affect of the Game
Player: Short-Term Effects of Highly and Mildly Aggressive
Video Games." *Personality and Social Psychology Bulletin,*
12;4 (December 1986): 390–402.

"At Last! Teenage Mutant Ninja Turtles is Released! History
and Hints of Those Hard-Shelled Crime Fighters." *Game
Player's Buyer's Guide: Nintendo Games,* 2;5 (1989): 8, 12, 14,
18, 23–24, 26.

*Bad Dudes Instruction Manual.* San Jose, Calif.: Data East,
1988.

Barthes, Roland. "Toys." Included in *Mythologies,* selected and
translated by Annette Lavers. Boston: Hill and Wang, 1972:
53–55.

Bateson, Gregory. "A Theory of Play and Fantasy." *Psychiatric
Research Reports* (American Psychiatric Association), 2
(1955): 39–51.

Becker, Ernest. *The Structure of Evil: An Essay on the Unification of the Science of Man.* New York: Braziller, 1968: 169–
176.

Berger, Peter. *The Social Construction of Reality: A Treatise on
the Sociology of Knowledge.* New York: Doubleday, 1967.

Bettelheim, Bruno. "The Importance of Play." *The Atlantic
Monthly,* March 1987: 35–46.

———— *The Uses of Enchantment: The Meaning and Importance of Fairy Tales.* New York: Knopf, 1976.

"Bionic Commando." *Game Player's Buyer's Guide to Nintendo Games,* 2;5: 42.

Bloom, Steve. *Video Invaders.* New York: Arco, 1982.

Bolter, J. David. *Turing's Man: Western Culture in the Computer Age.* Chapel Hill: The University of North Carolina Press, 1984.

Bowman, R. F., Jr. "A 'Pac-Man' Theory of Motivation: Tactical Implications for Classroom Instruction." *Educational Technology* (1982): 14–16.

Bowers, C. A. *The Cultural Dimensions of Educational Computing: Understanding the Non-Neutrality of Technology.* New York: Teachers College Press, 1980.

Braun, Claude, Georgette Goupil, Josette Giroux, and Yves Chagon. "Adolescents and Microcomputers: Sex Differences, Proxemics, Task and Stimulus Variables." *Journal of Psychology,* 120;6 (1986): 529–542.

Brooks, B. D. [Untitled.] In S. S. Baughman and P. D. Clagett, eds., "Video Games and Human Development: A Research Agenda for the '80s." Papers and Proceedings of the Symposium Held at Harvard Graduate School of Education, Cambridge, Massachusetts. Cambridge, Mass.: Gutman Library, Harvard Graduate School of Education, 1983.

Butler, M., and W. Paisley. *Woman and the Mass Media: Sourcebook for Research and Action.* New York: Human Sciences Press, 1980: 49–50.

Butterfield, F. "Video Game Specialists Come to Harvard to Praise Pac-Man, Not to Bury Him." *New York Times,* May 24, 1983: 22.

Carlon, Katherine, "Video Game Market Sharpens Focus." *Playthings* (June 1988): 30–31, 84–85.

Carlsson-Paige, Nancy, and Diane E. Levin. *The War Play Dilemma: Balancing Needs and Values in the Early Childhood Classroom.* New York: Teachers College Press, 1987.

———*Who's Calling the Shots? How to Respond Effectively to Children's Fascination with War Play and War Toys.* Philadelphia: New Society Publishers, 1990.

"Celebrity Profiles: Karch Kiralv." *Nintendo Power* (January/February 1989): 95.

Chaffin, J. D., B. Maxwell, and B. Thompson. "ARC-ED Curriculum: The Application of Video Game Format to Educational Software." *Exceptional Children,* 49 (1982): 173–178.

Chisholm, T. A., and P. Krishnakumar. "Are Computer Simulations Sexist?" *Simulation and Games,* 12;4 (1981): 379–392.

Clines, F. X. "Video Games Go Marching off to War." *New York Times,* February 17, 1982: 2–7.

Collins, G. "Video Games: A Diversion or a Danger?" *The New York Times,* February 17, 1983.

Cooper, Joel, and Diane Mackie. "Video Games and Aggression in Children." *Journal of Applied Social Psychology,* 16;8 726–744.

Csikszentmihayli, Mihaly. *Beyond Boredom and Anxiety.* San Francisco: Jossey Bass, 1975.

Davis, Philip J., and Reuben Hersch. *The Mathematical Experience.* Boston: Houghton Mifflin, 1981: 404.

Denison, D. C. "The Year of Playing Dangerously." *The Boston Globe Magazine,* December 8, 1985: 14–16, 99–107, 110.

Dominick, J. R. "Videogames, Television Violence, and Aggression in Teenagers." *Journal of Communication,* 34 (1984): 136–147.

"Double Dragon: Street Toughs Move to Attack." *Nintendo Power* (July–August 1988): 62–69.

"Double Dragon II: The Revenge." *Nintendo Power* (January/February 1990): 30–35.

Edelman, Lawrence. "MIT, Nintendo to Mix Playing with Teaching." *Boston Globe,* May 16, 1990.

Egli, E. A., and L. S. Meyers. "The Role of Video Game Playing in Adolescent Life: Is There Reason to be Concerned?" *Bulletin of the Psychonomic Society,* 22 (1984): 309–312.

Ehrmann, J. "Homo Ludens Revisited." In J. Ehrmann, ed., *Game, Play, Literature.* Boston: Beacon Press, 1968.

Ellis, Desmond. "Video Arcades, Youth, and Trouble." *Youth & Society,* 16;1 (September 1984): 47–65.

Ellis, Godfrey J. "Youth in the Electronic Environment: An Introduction." *Youth & Society,* 15;1 (September 1983): 3–12.

Engelhardt, T. "Saturday Morning Fever: The Hard Sell Take-over of Kids' TV." *Mother Jones,* 11;6 (1986): 38–48, 54.

Erikson, Erik H. *Toys and Reasons: Stages in the Ritualization of Experience.* New York: W. W. Norton, 1977: 43.

"Escape from the Prison Camp of Ordinary Games." *Game Player's Strategy Guide: Nintendo Games.* Greensboro, N.C.: Signal Publications, 1989: 21.

Faillois, R. *Man, Play, and Games.* New York: Schocken Books, 1979.

Favaro, P. J. "How Video Games Affect Players." *Softside,* 7;1 (1984): 16–17.

——"The Effects of Video Game Play on Mood, Physiological Arousal, and Psychomotor Performance." Ph.D. dissertation, Hofstra University, 1983.

Feinburg, S. G. *Combat in Child Art.* New York: W. W. Norton, 1973.

"Games That People Play." *Time,* January 18, 1982: 52.

Geertz, C. "Deep Play Notes on the Balinese Cockfight." *Daedalus* 101;1 (1972): 1–37.

Geertz, Clifford. "Thick Description: Toward an Interpretive Theory of Culture." In *The Interpretations of Cultures.* New York: Basic Books, 1973.

Gibb, G. D., J. R. Bailey, T. T. Lornbirth, and W. P. Wilson. "Personality Differences between High and Low Electronic Video Game Users." *Journal of Psychology,* 114 (1983): 143–152.

Givens, Ron. "Boys and Dolls in Toyland." *Newsweek,* November 27, 1989: 99–100.

Goffman, Erving. *Gender Advertisements.* New York: Harper and Row, 1976.

Graybill, Daniel, Janis R. Kirsch, and Edward E. Esselman. "Effects of Playing Violent versus Nonviolent Video Games on the Aggressive Ideation of Aggressive and Nonaggressive Children." *Child Study Journal,* 15;3 (1985): 199–205.

Graybill, Daniel, Marilyn Strawniak, Teri Hunter, and Margaret O'Leary. "Effects of Playing versus Observing Violent versus Nonviolent Video Games on Children's Aggression." *Psychology: A Quarterly Journal of Human Behavior,* 24;3 (1987): 1–8.

Greenberg, Bradley. "Gratification of Television Viewing and Their Correlates for British Children." In Jay Blumler and Elihu Katz, eds., *The Uses of Mass Communications*. Beverly Hills, Calif.: Sage, 1974: 71–92.

Greenblat, C. S. "Simulating Society." *Trans-Action*, 12;5 (1975): 48–52.

Greenfield, Patricia Marks. *Mind and Media: The Effects of Television, Video Games, and Computers*. Cambridge, Mass.: Harvard University Press, 1984.

———"Video Games and Cognitive Skills." In *Video Games and Human Development: A Research Agenda for the 80's*. Cambridge, Mass.: Harvard Graduate School of Education, 1983: 19–24.

Gutman, Dan. "Finding an Heir for Pac-Man." *Psychology Today*, 17 (March 1983): 10.

———"Video Games and National Character." *Psychology Today*, 17 (March 1983): 9.

Harris, Mary B., and Randall Williams. "Video Games and School Performance." *Education*, 105;3 (1984): 306–309.

Holland, Bill. "Nintendo to be Axed from Rental Bill." *Billboard Magazine*, 101 (April 29, 1989): 1.

Holsti, O. *Content Analysis for the Social Sciences and Humanities*. Reading, Mass.: Addison-Wesley, 1969.

Huizinga, J. *Homo Ludens*. Boston: Beacon Press, 1950.

Jones, Marshall B. "Video Games as Psychological Tests." *Simulation & Games*, 15;2 (June 1984): 131–157.

———"Videogame for Performance Testing." *American Journal of Psychology*, 94 (1981): 143–152.

Kaplan, S. J. "The Image of Amusement Arcades and Differences in Male and Female Video Game Playing." *Journal of Popular Culture*, 16 (1983): 93–98.

Kappes, Bruno M., and Dan L. Thompson. "Biofeedback vs. Video Games: Effects of Impulsivity, Locus of Control, and Self-Concept with Incarcerated Juveniles." *Journal of Clinical Psychology*, 41;5 (September 1985): 698–706.

Katz, Donald R. "The New Generation Gap." *Esquire Magazine*, February 1990: 49–50.

Katz, Elihu, Michael Gurevitch, and Hadassah Haas. "On the

Use of the Mass Media for Important Things," *American Sociological Review,* 38 (1973): 164–181.

Kegan, R. "Donkey Kong, Pac-Man, and the Meaning of Life: Reflections in River City." In *Video Games and Human Development: A Research Agenda for the 80's.* Cambridge, Mass.: Harvard Graduate School of Education, 1983: 4–7.

Kennedy, R. S., A. C. Bittner, Jr., and M. B. Jones. "Video-game and conventional tracking." *Perceptual and Motor Skills,* 53 (1981): 310.

Kerin, R., W. Lundstrom, and D. Sciglimpaglia. "Women in Advertisements: Retrospect and Prospect." *Journal of Advertising,* 8 (1979): 37–42.

Kerr, P. "Should Video Games be Restricted by Law?" *New York Times,* June 3, 1982: 1, 8.

Kestenbaum, Gerald I., and Lissa Weinstein. "Personality, Psychopathology, and Developmental Issues in Male Adolescent Game Use." *Journal of the American Academy of Child Psychiatry,* 24;3 (1985): 329–337.

Kiesler, S., L. Sproull, and J. S. Eccles. "Second Class Citizens." *Psychology Today,* 17;3 (1983): 41–48.

Klein, Martin H. "The Bite of Pac-Man." *Journal of Psychohistory,* 2;3 (Winter 1984): 395–401.

Koop, E. "Surgeon General Sees Danger in Video Games." *New York Times,* November 10, 1982: 16A.

Langway, L., et al. "Invasion of the Video Creatures." *Newsweek,* November 16, 1981: 90–94.

Lasch, Christopher. *The Culture of Narcissism.* New York: Norton, 1979.

Leccese, Donna. "Retailers Say Video Is a Dream Come True." *Playthings* (May 5, 1989): 32–33, 70–71.

———"Video Games Go Back to the Future." *Playthings* (June 1988): 32–33, 85–88.

Lockheed, Marlaine E. "Women, Girls, and Computers: A First Look at the Evidence." *Sex Roles,* 13;3/4 (1985): 115–122.

Loftus, Geoffrey R., and Elizabeth F. Loftus. *Mind at Play.* New York: Basic Books, 1983.

Lowery, B. R., and F. G. Knirk. "Micro-computer Video Games

and Spatial Visual Acquisition." *Journal of Educational Technology Systems,* 11 (1983): 155–166.

Lundstrom, W., and D. Sciglimpaglia. "Sex Portrayals in Advertising." *Journal of Marketing,* 41 (1977): 72–78.

Mackie, Diane, and Joel Cooper. "Gender and Computers: Two Surveys of Computer-related Attitudes." *Sex Roles,* 13;3/4 (1985): 215–228.

Malone, Thomas W. "Toward a Theory of Intrinsically Motivating Instruction." *Cognitive Science,* 5;4 (1981): 333–369.

————"What Makes Computer Games Fun?" BYTE, December 1981: 258–277.

————"What Makes Things Fun to Learn? A Study of Intrinsically Motivating Computer Games." Xerox Palo Alto Research Centre, Cognitive and Instructional Sciences Series (August 1980).

Marcus, Bill. "Preview *(Shinobi).*" *Game Pro Magazine* (1989): 24–25.

McClure, R. F., and F. G. Mears. "Video Game Players: Personality Characteristics and Demographic Variables." *Psychological Reports,* 55 (1984): 271–276.

McLuhan, Marshall. *Understanding Media: The Extensions of Man.* New York: McGraw-Hill, 1964.

Milgram, S. *Obedience to Authority.* New York: Harper and Row, 1974.

Mitchell, Edna. "The Dynamics of Family Interaction around Home Video Games." *Marriage and Family Review,* 8 (Spring 1985): 121–135.

Morlock, Henry, Todd Yando, and Karen Nigolean. "Motivation of Video Game Players." *Psychological Reports,* 57 (1985): 247–250.

National Coalition on Television Violence (NCTV). "Electronic Video Game Violence." *NCTV News,* 3 (February 3, 1982).

Needham, N. R. "The Impact of Video Games on American Youth." *Education Digest,* 48 (1983): 40–42.

————"Thirty Billion Quarters Can't be Wrong—Or Can They?" *Today's Education,* 71 (1982): 53–55.

Neisser, Ulrich. "Computers as Tools and as Metaphors." In

Charles Dechert, ed., *The Social Impact of Cybernetics*. Notre Dame, Ind.: University of Notre Dame Press, 1966.

Niehoff, Mariless S. "Psychological Perspectives: Computerized Children." *Elementary School Guidance and Counseling* (October 1983): 22–23.

*Nin-Ja Gaiden Instructions*. Tecmo, Inc., 1989.

"Nintendo Accused of Cornering Market." *Miami Herald,* December 9, 1989.

"Nintendo Expects Network with AT&T by 1991." *Television Digest,* August 21, 1989: 11.

"Nintendo Financial Network." *Television Digest,* October 9, 1989: 15.

"Nintendo Game of the Month: Ninja Gaiden." *Game Player's,* October 1989: 55.

"Nintendo Legal Battles." *Television Digest,* March 13, 1989: 17.

"Nintendo vs. Video Renters." *Television Digest,* August 14, 1989: 13.

Orwell, George. "Boys' Weeklies," included in *An Age Like This, 1920–1940*. In *The Collected Essays, Journalism, and Letters of George Orwell,* vol. 1, ed. Sonia Orwell and Ian Angus. New York: Harcourt, Brace and World, 1968: 460–485.

Paley, V. G. *Boys and Girls: Superheroes in the Doll Corner*. Chicago: University of Chicago Press, 1984.

Panelas, Tom. "Adolescents and Video Games: Consumption of Leisure and the Social Construction of the Peer Group." *Youth and Society,* 15;1 (September 1983): 51–65.

Papert, Seymour. *Mindstorms: Children, Computers, and Powerful Ideas*. New York: Basic Books, 1980.

*Platoon: Instruction Manual*. Wood Dale, Ill.: Sunsoft, 1988.

"*Playthings* Panel Peers into the 1990s." *Playthings,* May 5, 1989: 40–47.

"*Playthings* Retail Survey of Best-Selling Toys." *Playthings,* May 5, 1989: 22.

"Prepare Yourself for Conflict." *GamePro,* 2;3 (March 1990): 19.

Provenzo, Eugene F., Jr. *Beyond the Gutenberg Galaxy: Microcomputers and the Emergence of Post-Typographic Culture*. New York: Teachers College Press, 1986.

———"Toys: Remarks on Their Design and Function," included in the catalogue *Child's Play* (Lowe Art Museum, University of Miami, Coral Gables, Florida, March 8, 1979–April 15, 1979, and the Renwick Gallery of the National Collection of Fine Arts, Smithsonian Institution, Washington, D.C., June 15, 1979–September 9, 1979). Coral Gables, Fla.: Lowe Art Museum, The University of Miami, 1979: 9–15.

Provenzo, Eugene F., Jr., and Arlene Brett. *The Complete Block Book*. Syracuse, N.Y.: Syracuse University Press, 1983.

"Rampage." *Game Player's Buyer's Guide to Nintendo Games,* 2;5: 66.

Rich, Jason R. "Face to Face with Danny Pintauro." *Game Player's,* October 1989: 25.

Roberts, J. M., and B. Sutton-Smith. "The Cross-Cultural and Psychological Study of Games." *International Review of Sport Sociology,* 6 (1971): 79–87.

Robinson, John. "Television and Leisure Time: A New Scenario." *Journal of Communication,* 31;1 (Winter 1981): 120–130.

"RoboCop." Advertisement included on the back cover of *Game Player's* magazine, October 1989.

Salas, Teresa. "Video Game Market Continues to Shine." *Playthings,* January 1990: 38ff.

Saraf, M. J. "Semiotic Signs in Sport Activity." *International Review of Sport Sociology,* 12;2 (1977): 89–102.

Schwartz, Steven. *Compute's Guide to Nintendo Games*. Radnor, Pa.: Compute! Books, 1989.

Selnow, G. W. "Playing Videogames: The Electronic Friend." *Journal of Communication,* 34 (1984): 148–156.

Silvern, Steven B., and Peter A. Williamson. "The Effects of Video Game Play on Young Children's Aggression, Fantasy, and Prosocial Behavior." *Journal of Applied Developmental Psychology,* 8 (October–December, 1987): 453–462.

Skow, J., et al. "Games That Play People." *Time,* January 18, 1982: 50–58.

Sloan, Douglas. "For the Record." *Teachers College Record,* 85;4 (Summer 1984): 539–547.

Snyder, Benson. *The Hidden Curriculum*. Cambridge, Mass.: MIT Press, 1971.

Sutton-Smith, Brian. *Toys as Culture*. New York: Gardner Press, 1986.

Sutton-Smith, Brian, and J. B. Roberts. "Rubrics of Competitive Behavior." *Journal of Genetic Psychology* 105 (1964): 13–37.

Swedish Information Service. "War Toys." *Social Change in Sweden*, 9 (September 1980): 5.

"There's No Match for WWF Wrestlemania." Full-page advertisement, *Game Player's*, June/July 1989: 9.

"Thundercade." Advertisement included in *Game Player's Strategy Guide: Nintendo Games*. Greensboro, N.C.: Signal Publications, 1989: 37.

Timnik, L. "Electronic Bullies." *Psychology Today*, February 1982: 10–15.

Toles, Terri. "Video Games and American Military Ideology." In *The Critical Communications Review, Vol. III: Popular Culture and Media Events*, ed. Vincent Mosco and Janet Wasko. Norwood, N.J.: Ablex, 1985: 207–223.

"Top 30." *Nintendo Power*, November/December 1989: 31.

Trinkaus, J. W. "Arcade Video Games: An Informal Look." *Psychological Reports*, 52 (1983): 586.

Tuna, Thomas. "Video Games Continue Their Strong Play." *Playthings*, May 5, 1989: 34–35, 72–73.

Turkle, Sherry. *The Second Self: Computers and the Human Spirit*. New York: Simon and Schuster, 1984.

———"The Subjective Computer: Study in the Psychology of Personal Computation." *Social Studies of Science*, 12 (1982): 173–205.

———"They Zap, Crackle, and Pop, but Video Games Can be Powerful Tools for Learning." *People*, May 31, 1982: 74, 79.

"Twin Cobra." *GamePro*, 2;3 (March 1990): 55.

"Videogames—Fun or Serious Threat?" *U.S. News and World Report*, February 22, 1982: 7.

"The Wait Is Over. Power Glove and U-Force Debut!" *Game Player's Strategy Guide*. Greensboro, N.C.: Signal Research, 1989: 124.

Wanner, E. "The Electronic Bogeyman." *Psychology Today,* October 1982: 8–11.

Ware, Mary Catherine, and Mary Frances Stuck. "Sex-Role Messages vis-à-vis Microcomputer Use: A Look at the Pictures." *Sex Roles,* 13;3/4 (1985): 205–214.

Weibel, K. *Mirror, Mirror: Images of Women Reflected in Popular Culture.* Garden City, N.Y.: Anchor Books, 1977.

Weizenbaum, Joseph. *Computer Power and Human Reason: From Judgement to Calculation.* San Francisco: W. H. Freeman, 1979.

Wilder, Gita, Diane Mackie, and Joel Cooper. "Gender and Computers: Two Surveys of Computer-Related Attitudes." *Sex Roles,* 13;3/4 (1985): 215–228.

Williams, Frederick. *The Communications Revolution.* Beverly Hills, Calif.: Sage Publications, 1982.

Wilson, Mike. "The Wizard of Nintendo." *Miami Herald,* March 12, 1990: 1–2C.

Winner, Langdon. *Autonomous Technology.* Cambridge, Mass.: MIT Press, 1977.

Winnicott, D. W. *Playing and Reality.* New York: Basic Books, 1971.

Winograd, Terry, and Fernando Flores. *Understanding Computers and Cognition: A New Foundation for Design.* Reading, Mass.: Addison-Wesley, 1987.

Witowsky, K. "Up in Arms over Guns in Toyland." *Mother Jones,* 11;3 (1986): 12.

# Index